Dear Mr. Longfellow

Dear Mr. Longfellow

LETTERS TO AND FROM THE CHILDREN'S POET

Sydelle Pearl

 **Prometheus Books**

59 John Glenn Drive
Amherst, New York 14228–2119

Published 2012 by Prometheus Books

Cover images:
Longfellow portrait reproduced courtesy of the Print Collection, Miriam and Ira D. Wallach Division of Art, Prints and Photographs, the New York Public Library, Astor, Lenox and Tilden Foundations
Letters reproduced by permission of the Houghton Library, Harvard University, call number bMS Am 1340.7

Cover design by Nicole Sommer-Lecht

Inquiries should be addressed to
Prometheus Books
59 John Glenn Drive
Amherst, New York 14228–2119
VOICE: 716–691–0133 • FAX: 716–691–0137
WWW.PROMETHEUSBOOKS.COM

16 15 14 13 12   5 4 3 2 1

Printed in the United States of America on acid-free paper

Henry Wadsworth Longfellow in his library at Craigie House, Cambridge. Photo from an 1882 engraving by Samuel Hollyer. Courtesy National Park Service, Longfellow House–Washington's Headquarters National Historic Site.

In memory of my mother, Ruth Kaplan Pearl,
poet and playwright,
and my father, David Pearl,
who recited Longfellow's "The Arrow and the Song."

Contents

CONTENTS

Introduction

"Thank you so much
for writing for children
as well as grown folks,
it makes us feel that
we are not forgotten."

Figure I.1. Henry Wadsworth Longfellow, 1879. [A.5308.96
Nine Portraits of Longfellow, 1842–1879 . . .] Courtesy of the Trustees of the
Boston Public Library / Rare Books.

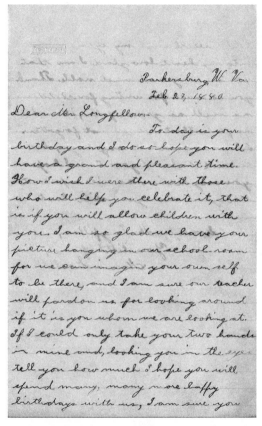

Figure I.2. Photograph of Nannie Gould's letter, page 1. [bMS Am 1340.7 Houghton Library, Harvard University.]

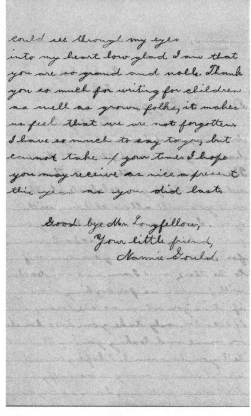

could see through my eyes
into my heart how glad I am that
you are so grand and noble. Thank
you so much for writing for children
as well as grown folks, it makes
us feel that we are not forgotten.
I have so much to say to you, but
cannot take up your time. I hope
you may receive as nice a present
this year as you did last.

Good-bye Mr. Longfellow,
Your little friend,
Nannie Gould.

Figure I.3. Photograph of Nannie Gould's letter, page 2. [bMS Am 1340.7 Houghton Library, Harvard University.]

Parkersburg, W. Va.
[West Virginia]
Feb. 27, 1880

Dear Mr. Longfellow:—

To-day is your birthday and I do so hope you will have a grand and pleasant time. How I wish I were there with those who will help you celebrate it, that is if you will allow children with you. I am so glad we have your picture hanging in our school-room for we can imagine your own self to be there, and I am sure our teacher will pardon us for looking around if it is you whom we are looking at. If I could only take your two hands in mine and, looking you in the eyes tell you how much I hope you will spend many, many more happy birthdays with us, I am sure you could see through my eyes into my heart how glad I am that you are so grand and noble. Thank you so much for writing for children as well as grown folks, it makes us feel that we are not forgotten. I have so much to say to you, but cannot take up your time. I hope you may receive as nice a present this year as you did last.

Good-bye Mr. Longfellow,
Your little friend,
Nannie Gould.[1]

*T*ake a look at the picture at the beginning of this book. If you were going to school in the 1880s, this is one of the faces you would probably see looking down at you from the wall of your classroom. Who was Henry Wadsworth Longfellow and how did he come to be so loved, especially in the minds and hearts of children?

The answer begins in the year 1839 with the story of a particular horse chestnut tree that grew next to a blacksmith's shop on Brattle Street in Cambridge, Massachusetts. The poet Henry Wadsworth Long-fellow lived in a big yellow house on Brattle Street and walked by the blacksmith's shop and the tree on his way to work at Harvard College, where he was pro-fessor of modern languages.

In those days, people traveled by horse and car-riage. The blacksmith's shop was the place where horses could be fitted with strong iron shoes to protect their hooves as they carried people around Cambridge and beyond. It was also the place where axes, pitchforks, pots, pans, and other household objects were made and mended. The blacksmith needed certain tools to work with, such as an anvil, a hammer, and a fire or forge that melted iron down to the desired shape. His shop was a very busy and important place in the community.

Henry noticed how the children loved to watch the blacksmith, Dexter Pratt, work his magic with the forge, and on October 5, 1839, he wrote a poem titled "The Village Blacksmith." The poem was published in a book called *Ballads and Other Poems* in 1841 and became very well known, especially among school-children, who learned to recite it.

"The Village Blacksmith"

Under a spreading chestnut-tree
    The village smithy stands;
The smith, a mighty man is he,
    With large and sinewy hands;
And the muscles of his brawny arms
    Are strong as iron bands.

His hair is crisp and black, and long,
    His face is like the tan;
His brow is wet with honest sweat,
    He earns whate'er he can,
And looks the whole world in the face,
    For he owes not any man.

Week in, week out, from morn till night,
    You can hear his bellows blow;
You can hear him swing his heavy sledge,
    With measured beat and slow,
Like a sexton ringing the village bell,
    When the evening sun is low.

And children coming home from school
    Look in at the open door;
They love to see the flaming forge,
    And hear the bellows roar.
And catch the burning sparks that fly
    Like chaff from a threshing-floor.

He goes on Sunday to the Church,
    And sits among his boys;
He hears the parson pray and preach,

He hears his daughter's voice,
Singing in the village choir,
   And it makes his heart rejoice.

It sounds to him like her mother's voice,
   Singing in Paradise!
He needs must think of her once more,
   How in the grave she lies;
And with his hard, rough hand he wipes
   A tear out of his eyes.

Toiling, —rejoicing, —sorrowing,
   Onward through life he goes;
Each morning sees some task begin,
   Each evening sees it close;
Something attempted, something done,
   Has earned a night's repose.

Thanks, thanks to thee, my worthy friend,
   For the lesson thou hast taught!
Thus at the flaming forge of life
   Our fortunes must be wrought;
Thus on its sounding anvil shaped
   Each burning deed and thought.[2]

Henry lived for another forty-one years after the poem was published and went on to write many other poems, but "The Village Blacksmith" remained one of the most favorite poems of the people.

Figure I.4. Henry Wadsworth Longfellow, 1842. [A.5308.96 *Nine Portraits of Longfellow, 1842–1879 . . .*] Courtesy of the Trustees of the Boston Public Library/Rare Books.

By the time children began writing to him and celebrating his birthday in the 1880s, many of their grandparents, parents, principals, and teachers had already learned this poem at their own schools!

H. W. Longfellow. esq.

I am overjoyed with happiness I spoke for the first time in my life at our school I spoke one of your Poems subject the village Blacksmith In Honor of your Birthday and I succeeded very well I wish you many happy returns of your Birthday you don't know how much we think of your Beautiful Poems we couldnt do without them I hope when I am a man I will see you and shake hands with you My Dear Dear Mr. H. W. Longfellow.

    Robert Farrar. St. Paul Minn.
    Feb. 28th. 1882
    Robert Farrar.
    10 ½ years old.
    Address.
    596. Princes Block
    Jackson St. St. Paul
    Minn. [Minnesota]

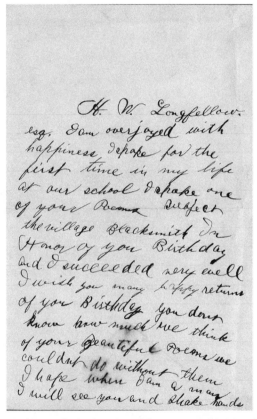

Figure I.5. Photograph of Robert Farrar's letter, page 1. [bMS Am 1340.7 Houghton Library, Harvard University.]

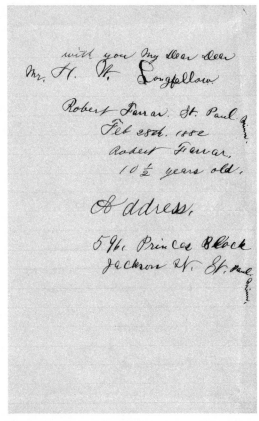

Figure I.6. Photograph of Robert Farrar's letter, page 2. [bMS Am 1340.7 Houghton Library, Harvard University.]

During his lifetime, Henry received over six thousand letters from relatives, friends, and strangers who enjoyed reading his poetry.[3] His poems were read, recited, and sung in schools and homes across the United States of America. They were translated into different languages and known throughout the world. Between the years 1880 and 1882, when Henry was seventy-three to seventy-five years old, he received 786 birthday greetings, many of them from children.[4] Portraits of other famous American writers such as John Greenleaf Whittier and Oliver Wendell Holmes adorned the classroom walls,[5] but only Henry Wadsworth Longfellow was called "the children's poet."[6] The birthday letters came from all over America and other countries too. Henry did his best to answer them. Two of the letters that Henry wrote to children appear in this book.

Henry was so famous that mail carriers knew where he lived in Cambridge, Massachusetts, even though the letters listed his name, city, and state, but no street address. In 1880, the City of Cambridge was one of the branches of the Boston post office, and two or three mail deliveries were made daily.[7]

Pictures of Henry and the Longfellow House were featured on many prints that appeared in magazines.[8] There were even jugs with Henry's portrait that people bought in stores.[9]

Figure I.7. Photograph of Kéramos jug (LONG 5829). Henry's poem, "Kéramos," appears on the other side of the jug. Courtesy National Park Service, Longfellow House—Washington's Headquarters National Historic Site.

Some people confused Henry with the famous poet and playwright William Shakespeare, who had written in the 1600s! Henry once wrote to Annie Fields, the wife of his publisher, James, "A stranger called here and asked if Shakespeare lived in this neighborhood. I told him I knew no such person. Do you?"[10]

Children felt very comfortable with Henry, and he welcomed them warmly to his home. Annie Fields recalled that one little boy often came to see him. During a visit, the boy looked at the many books in Henry's library and asked if he owned *Jack the Giant Killer*. When Henry said no, the child got off his lap and left the house only to return the next morning with two cents so that Henry could go buy his own copy of the book![11]

Eleanor Hallowell Abbott wrote about visiting with Henry when she was a child in her book *Being Little in Cambridge When Everyone Else Was Big*. She went with her friends along Brattle Street just in time to meet Henry when he took his late-afternoon walk. Henry would hug the children and invite them to his home. According to Eleanor, "we went back with Mr. Longfellow into his beautiful house and library, where urging him as discreetly as possible into the depths of his big chair we took turns sitting in his lap, while he talked *our* kind of talk to us about practical things such as kittens and rabbits and sleds and skates."[12]

Most of the children who wrote to Henry were eight to sixteen years old. The photographed letters in this book appear as the children wrote them from their schools or homes, where they also celebrated his birthday. Some letters contain cross-outs, spelling, or grammatical errors that have not been corrected so you can see how children wrote about one hundred thirty years ago. Clarifying information, such as the name of a state, appears in brackets. Penmanship was an important subject taught in school. Children needed to learn how to write because that was the main way people communicated.

The letters were written before inventions we take for granted, such as the airplane, automobile, refrigerator, radio, television, copy machine, cell phone, and computer. They were written before child labor laws were passed. While many children were writing to Henry from their schools, many other children were not going to school at all. They were busy working long hours in factories, mills, farms, or mines. It wasn't until 1938 that a national law was signed by President Franklin Delano Roosevelt making it illegal for children under the age of sixteen to work.[13]

In the South, former slaves established schools after the Civil War, but many black people could not read or write.[14] There were separate teacher-training programs for white and black students, and white children and black children attended separate schools.[15] In Alabama, for example, the 1878 school report stated, "In no case shall it be lawful to unite in one school both colored and white children."[16] It wasn't until the 1954 United States Supreme Court decision in *Brown v. Board of Education* that segregated schools in the United States were outlawed.[17]

The students who wrote to Henry knew how much he liked children. By the time they began sending him birthday wishes, he was a grandfather. He was used to being with children all of his life. Henry was the second oldest in a family with four boys and four girls. When Henry became a father, he had two sons and four daughters. One of his daughters, Fanny, died when she was very small. When children wrote to tell him about their lives, Henry must have thought about his own children. In their letters, children said that they wanted to visit him, and others wrote to thank him for prior visits to his house. Henry wrote in his journal on June 13, 1880, about one of these visits, "Yesterday I had a visit from two schools; some sixty girls and boys, in all. It seems to give them so much pleasure, that it gives me pleasure."[18]

Some of the children in the photograph have slates in front of them. They were like small blackboards. Children would write in chalk on the slate and then transfer their work onto paper with a pencil or a quill pen. Can you imagine children sitting at their desks and writing to Henry during the years 1880–1882?

Figure I.8. Photograph of children in third-grade Boston class (Primary Class III, Wells District) by A. H. Folsom in 1892. Courtesy of the Boston Public Library, Print Department.

Chapter 1

"Tell me of something
you did when you was a boy."

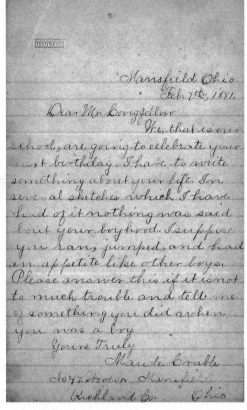

Figure 1.1. Photograph of Maude Crable's letter. [bMS Am 1340.7 Houghton Library, Harvard University.]

Mansfield, Ohio
Feb 7th, 1881.

Dear Mr. Longfellow

We, that is our school,
are going to celebrate your next birthday. I have to write
something about your life. In several sketches which I
have had of it nothing was said about your boyhood. I
suppose you ran, jumped, and had an appetite like other
boys. Please answer this if it is not to much trouble and
tell me of something you did when you was a boy.

Yours Truly
Maude Crable
No. 47 Wood St.   Mansfield,
Richland Co.   Ohio

*H*enry Wadsworth Longfellow was born in Portland, Massachusetts, on February 27, 1807, the second child of Zilpah Wadsworth and Stephen Longfellow. In 1820, Maine was declared an independent state. By the time Henry was twelve years old, there were eight siblings in all. The children made up a rhyme with everyone's name: "Stephen and Henry / Elizabeth and Anne / Alex and Mary / Ellen and Sam."[1]

Henry lived in the house his grandfather, General Peleg Wadsworth, a Revolutionary War veteran, had built. His mother, Zilpah, had grown up there with her seven brothers and two sisters.[2] One sister, Henry's aunt Lucia, and two servants, lived with Henry's family and helped with the bustling household.[3] Zilpah loved to play the piano, and in the evening, the children and their friends would sing along to the music.[4] Henry learned to play the piano and flute when he was a boy.[5]

There was a garden in the back of the house. All his life, Henry loved flowers, especially lilacs.[6]

The house wasn't far from the sea, and Henry saw many ships come into port. There was the mill, where strong ropes were woven for ships. There was the pottery, where the clay was shaped into pitchers and bowls by the potter's hands. There was Deering's Woods, where Henry might have gathered acorns. Cows grazed during the day in pasturing fields, and boys led the cows back to each family's barn in the evening. The streets echoed with the voice of the town crier who called out the news.[7]

When Henry was well established as a poet, he recalled "that dear old town" in a poem called "My Lost Youth." Here are the first three verses and the last verse:

"My Lost Youth"

Often I think of the beautiful town
    That is seated by the sea;
Often in thought go up and down
The pleasant streets of that dear old town,
    And my youth comes back to me.
        And a verse from a Lapland song
        Is haunting my memory still:
        "A boy's will is the wind's will,
And the thoughts of youth are long, long thoughts."

I can see the shadowy lines of its trees,
    And catch, in sudden gleams,
The sheen of the far-surrounding seas,
And islands that were the Hesperides
    Of all my boyish dreams.

And the burden of that old song,
It murmurs and whispers still:
"A boy's will is the wind's will,
And the thoughts of youth are long, long thoughts."

I remember the black wharves and the slips,
And the sea-tides tossing free;
And Spanish sailors with bearded lips,
And the beauty and mystery of the ships,
And the magic of the sea.
And the voice of that wayward song
Is singing and saying still:
"A boy's will is the wind's will,
And the thoughts of youth are long, long thoughts." . . .

And Deering's Woods are fresh and fair,
And with joy that is almost pain
My heart goes back to wander there,
And among the dreams of the days that were,
I find my lost youth again.
And the strange and beautiful song,
The groves are repeating it still:
"A boy's will is the wind's will,
And the thoughts of youth are long, long thoughts."[8]

15 Evans St. Mt. Auburn.

Cincinnati Ohio. Feb. 3,rd 1880

Henry W. Longfellow.

Dear Sir:

You have probally learned from other sources the fact of the celebration of your coming birthday, by the public schools of Cincinnati.

As I left Massachusetts only a year ago, and my parents, in their early years, lived near Portland, Me., I assure you that I feel it an honor to be selected to write a sketch of your life.

But you must know we boys and girls would like to know something about you when you was a boy, and this we cannot find in books.

If it is not asking too much, will you do me the favor to write me something about your school-boy and college days? Any little incident would be interesting to us.

I hope dear sir, I have not asked too much of you. But you know, "A boy's will is the wind's will"

And the thoughts of youth are long long thoughts I am twelve years old but have read with pleasure your poems and enjoy looking at your faithful portrait hanging on our walls.   Eugene W. Mann

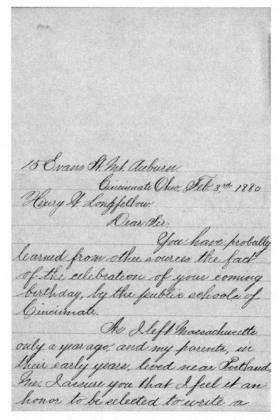

15 Evans St. Mt. Auburn.
Cincinnati Ohio, Feb. 3rd 1880
Henry W. Longfellow.
Dear Sir.
You have probably
learned from other sources the fact
of the celebration of your coming
birthday, by the public schools of
Cincinnati.
As I left Massachusetts
only a year ago, and my parents, in
their early years, lived near Portland,
Me. I assure you that I feel it an
honor to be selected to write a

Figure 1.2. Photograph of Eugene W. Mann's letter, page 1. [bMS Am 1340.7 Houghton Library, Harvard University.]

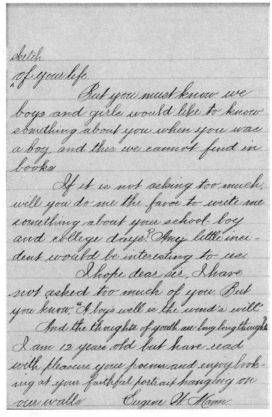

sketch
of your life.
⌃
But you must know we boys and girls would like to know something about you when you was a boy, and this we cannot find in books

If it is not asking too much, will you do me the favor to write me something about your school-boy and college days? Any little incident would be interesting to us

I hope dear sir, I have not asked too much of you. But you know, "A boy's will is the wind's will And the thoughts of youth are long long thoughts"

I am 12 years old but have read with pleasure your poems and enjoy looking at your faithful portrait hanging on our walls   Eugene W. Mann

Figure 1.3. Photograph of Eugene W. Mann's letter, page 2. [bMS Am 1340.7 Houghton Library, Harvard University.]

Henry's father was a lawyer who often traveled away from home to the General Court of Massachusetts in Boston. His law office was in Portland.[9] Stephen Longfellow was also chief fire warden for the town. In 1815, when Henry was eight, Stephen found himself calling out orders to put out the fire on the roof of his own house! Their kitchen servant had made the fire in the hearth too hot. The roof was badly damaged. Before replacing it, Stephen decided to have a third floor built on the house to accommodate his growing family.[10] After the renovations were complete, Henry slept in a bedroom on the third floor, sharing it with his older brother, Stephen.[11]

Can you imagine Henry looking out one of the windows as a child?

Figure 1.4. Line drawing of Wadsworth-Longfellow House,
circa 1876, by John B. Hudson Jr. for Edward H. Elwell's publication
"Portland and Vicinity" (1876). Collections of Maine Historical Society. Coll.
2113/M P837.13 1876.

When Henry was three years old, he went to a private school where he was taught by Mrs. Fellows.[12] At the age of five, Henry studied with Mr. N. H. Carter at another private school, and when his teacher moved to the Portland Academy, so did Henry. He was five years and four months old when his teacher wrote: "Master Henry Longfellow is one of the best boys we have in school. He spells and reads very well. He can also add and multiply numbers. His conduct this quarter was very correct and amiable. N. H. Carter. June 30, 1813."[13]

At the age of twelve, Henry began keeping a copy-book with some of his own riddles and early poems. Henry studied reading, penmanship, Bible, arithmetic, declamation [recitation], spelling, Latin, and Greek at the Portland Academy.[14] Here is a rhyme he wrote in school on November 17, 1819.

> **There's not a Lady in the land**
> **But hath twenty nails on each hand**
> **Five and twenty on hands and feet**
> **And this is true without deceit.**[15]

He was reading books like *The Arabian Nights* and *Robinson Crusoe*.[16] On Sunday, everyone took turns reading from the Bible when Zilpah gathered the family around her. They all walked to the First Parish Church in the morning and then again for the afternoon service.[17] The poetry and rhythm of the hymns must have left an impression upon Henry.

At the age of thirteen, Henry wrote a poem called "The Battle of Lovell's Pond" about the Revolutionary War. He signed it "Henry" and secretly brought it to the office of the *Portland Gazette*, telling only his sister Anne how he hoped it would be published.[18] It was printed in the next edition! While visiting a friend that evening, Henry was crushed to hear his friend's father criticize the poem. He excused himself quickly and wept until he fell asleep.[19] But he kept on writing poetry.

When Henry was fourteen and Stephen was sixteen, they were both admitted to Bowdoin College in Brunswick, Maine, but their parents thought that they were too young to live away from home. One year later, they rented rooms at a preacher's house because there was no more space in the dormitory.[20] Henry and Stephen were homesick and planned to make a surprise visit home for Thanksgiving. They must have felt so disappointed to find that there weren't any horses and carriages available, even though they had put in a reservation![21]

Now they missed home even more. They spent the holiday at the home of one of the professors. The two brothers received this letter from their father:

> *On Wednesday the children were all on tiptoe, and the window seats were filled everytime a chaise passed. We waited dinner some time, & ma kept some tidbits for you by the fire until night, and our tea was delayed to a late hour. But when P. Greenleaf arrived with the unwelcome tidings that you were not coming, the disappointment was visible in every countenance, & poor Alexander could not suppress his tears. You see, my dear children how much we are all interested in everything that concerns you and how tenderly we love you.[22]*

In time, the two brothers began to enjoy college life. Their days started early with six o'clock prayers in the chapel. Although it was against the rules, Stephen spent many evenings at a nearby tavern eating late suppers.[23] Henry was more studious than his brother. He liked taking long walks with his new friends in the forests surrounding the school.[24] He liked belonging to a literary society and discovering new books to read.[25] Henry especially loved *The Sketch Book* by Washington Irving.[26] He was excited to have some of his poems published in the *United States Literary Gazette*.[27] But Henry worried about what he would do when he finished college. He knew he wanted to be a writer. Henry wrote a letter to his father his senior year that said:

> *[T]he fact is—and I will not disguise it in the least, for I think I ought not,—the fact is, I most eagerly aspire after future eminence in literature, my whole soul burns most ardently after it, and every earthly thought centers in it.*[28]

Henry wrote that he wished to spend one year at Harvard College in Cambridge, Massachusetts, reading and studying literature. His father agreed to the one year of study but felt that Henry should become a lawyer so he could make a living.

A wonderful thing happened after Henry graduated from Bowdoin in 1825, in a class of thirty-seven students.[29] The college elected to create a new position, professor of modern languages, and Henry was offered the job! He was expected to travel to Europe to learn the languages and literature that he would then teach to his students. Henry studied law in his father's office in the Portland house before traveling across the ocean by ship in the spring of 1826.[30] His father paid for his journey.[31] Henry was away in France, Spain, Italy, and Germany for the next three years. His mother wrote to him just after he began his travels.

> *I will not say how much we miss your elastic step, your cheerful voice, your melodious flute, but will say farewell, my dear son, may God be with and prosper you.*[32]

Henry must have thought of the sailors that he remembered when he was a boy growing up near the sea in Portland. Now he would have his own adventures!

Chapter 2

*"I hope when I am a man
I can write books."*

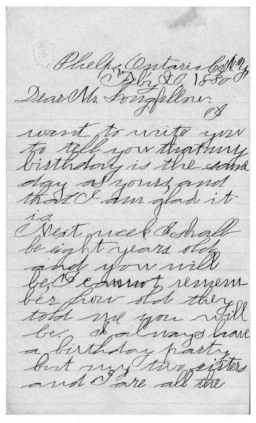

Figure 2.1. Photograph of Beecher S. Bowdish's letter, page 1.
[bMS Am 1340.7 Houghton Library, Harvard University.]

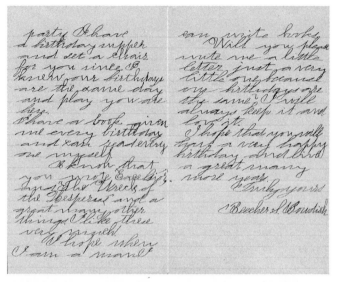

Figure 2.2. Photograph of Beecher S. Bowdish's letter, page 2. [bMS Am 1340.7 Houghton Library, Harvard University.]

Phelps Ontario Co. N.Y. [New York]
Feb'y 20, 1880

Dear Mr. Longfellow:

I want to write you to tell you that my birthday is the same day as yours, and that I am glad it is.

Next week I shall be eight years old and you will be, I cannot remember how old they told me you will be. I always have a birthday party but my two sisters and I are all the party. I have a birthday supper and set a chair for you since I knew our birthdays are the same day and play you are here.

I have a book given me every birthday and can read every one myself.

I know that you wrote "Excelcior" and "The Wreck of the Hesperus" and a great many other things. I like these very much.

I hope when I am a man I can write books.

Will you please write me a little letter just a very little one because our birthdays are the same? I will always keep it and love it.

I hope that you will have a very happy birthday and live a great many more years.

Truly yours
Beecher S. Bowdish

*H*enry attended university lectures, studied with tutors, and spent time in libraries reading the literature of the countries he visited while staying in hotels or with native families.[1] Most of all, Henry enjoyed learning languages by walking through the streets and countryside, carrying his flute in his knapsack, speaking with people he met along the way.[2] They shared their stories and songs with him.

In the French village of Auteuil, he attended a festival in midsummer that was held in honor of the patron saint of the village. Henry's eyes must have grown wide to see "the strolling players, and rope-dancers, and jugglers, and giants, and dwarfs, and wild beasts."[3]

In Spain, Henry's balcony on the third floor of a house overlooked the busy streets of the main square of Puerta Del Sol in the city of Madrid. There was a peasant selling gobbling turkeys, another selling watermelon, still another selling watercress, and a woman wearing a blue kerchief selling clucking, fluttering chickens. Each peddler had a different chant.[4] Meanwhile, there was the "rumbling of wheels, the clatter of hoofs, and the clang of church-bells."[5]

In Madrid, Henry was happy to meet his favorite author, Washington Irving, busily writing about the life of Christopher Columbus.[6]

In Rome, Henry saw a man holding out his hat and, since he looked poor (he was wearing a thread-bare coat), Henry put some money into his hat. The man was insulted at being taken for a beggar! He dumped out the coins and pulled the hat down over his head tightly, covering his ears, and walked away in a huff![7]

While Henry was eating breakfast one morning at an inn in the Italian village of La Riccia, an affec-tionate spaniel with mournful eyes came up to him. Henry asked about the dog's owner and was told that he had been hanged for killing and robbing people of the Abruzzi Mountains. Henry wondered about the stories the dog would tell if it could only talk![8]

Henry was learning to speak the languages of the countries he visited and to read other languages too. In a letter home he wrote:

With the French and Spanish languages, I am familiarly conversant, so as to speak them correctly, and write them with as much ease and fluency as I do the English. The Portuguese I read without difficulty. And with regard to my proficiency in the Italian, I have only to say that all at the hotel where I lodge took me for an Italian until I told them I was an American.[9]

The years passed quickly. In 1830, he became chair of Modern Languages at Bowdoin College and also served as the part-time librarian. In 1831 he married Mary Storer Potter of Portland, and they settled down happily in Brunswick, Maine. During the next few years, he translated the poems of foreign poets and wrote and published textbooks in Spanish, French, and Italian to use with his students.[10] He was also writing a book of his experiences abroad called *Outre-Mer*, French for "Beyond the Sea."

Figure 2.3. Painting of Mary Storer Potter Longfellow by
Augustus Vincent Tack. Collections of Maine Historical Society. A90-209.

Henry and Mary weren't settled long, however, when Henry was invited to become professor of modern languages at Harvard College. Once again, Henry set sail for Europe, this time with his wife. He was planning to master his German and to study Swedish, Danish, and Dutch. But sorrow awaited him. Mary died in Rotterdam, the Netherlands, on November 29, 1835, from an infection caused by a miscarriage.[11] Henry wrote a poem about her called "Footsteps of Angels."[12]

He stayed in Germany and tried to read and study while he mourned her death. He was so sad that he could not concentrate. To take his mind off his troubles, Henry decided to travel through Switzerland where he "stood all alone at the tops of the great mountains."[13] In Interlaken, he met Boston merchant Nathan Appleton, who was traveling with his daughters, Fanny and Mary; their brother, Tom; and their cousin, William.[14] Henry especially enjoyed spending time with nineteen-year-old Fanny and was sorry when he had to return to America.

Henry came to Cambridge, Massachusetts, in the

fall of 1836. He lived on the third floor of a house on Kirkland Street with other professors.[15] He made new friends like Cornelius Felton, professor of Greek and future president of Harvard, and Charles Sumner, librarian at the law school and future senator. They socialized together with two other friends and called themselves "The Five of Clubs."[16] Henry was an elegant dresser like his friend Charles and wore colorful waistcoats (vests) and cravats (ties). He even wore a pair of lavender gloves![17]

In 1837, Henry was searching for a new place to live. He went to see the widow Craigie at 105 Brattle Street in Cambridge to see if he could rent a room in her big yellow house. Andrew Craigie had been a general in the Revolutionary War and a rich man, but he died leaving many debts. His widow, Elizabeth, needed to earn extra money by taking in boarders. The house was well known in the area because it had once been the headquarters of George Washington, from 1775 to 1776 at the beginning of the American Revolution. His wife, Martha, had visited him there.

When Mrs. Craigie answered the door, she looked

at Henry's bright clothing and assumed he must be a student. She told him that he couldn't rent a room. Henry explained that he was a professor and an author. When she pointed to his own book, *Outre-Mer; A Pilgrimage beyond the Sea*, on one of her side tables, Henry knew he would be able to rent a room at Craigie House after all![18]

Chapter 3

"Tell me the names
of your daughters
and if they are all living."

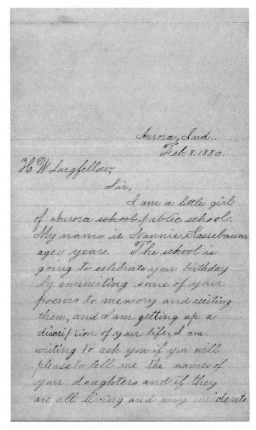

Figure 3.1. Photograph of Nannie Kassebaum's letter, page 1.
[bMS Am 1340.7 Houghton Library, Harvard University.]

Figure 3.2. Photograph of Nannie Kassebaum's letter, page 2.
[bMS Am 1340.7 Houghton Library, Harvard University.]

Aurora, Ind [Indiana]
Feb. 8. 1880

HWLongfellow,

Sir,

I am a little girl of Aurora ~~school~~ *public school. My name is Nannie Kassebaum age 11 years. The school is going to celebrate your birthday by committing some of your poems to memory and reciting them, and I am getting up a discription of your life. I am writing to ask you if you will please to tell me the names of your daughters and if they are all living and any incidents of your life that would be interesting to the school.*

Yours Respectfully,
Nannie Kassebaum

*H*enry never forgot Fanny Appleton of Beacon Hill and spent considerable time courting her over the next seven years. He even wrote a novel called *Hyperion* in which he described a couple named Paul Fleming and Mary Ashburton who were really Henry and Fanny in disguise.[1] Finally, when

Fanny sent Henry a letter saying that she agreed to marry him, Henry was so happy that tears came to his eyes, and he hurried to her house, 39 Beacon Street, on foot, "with the speed of an arrow—too restless to sit in a carriage."[2] On July 13, 1843, they were married. In the meantime, the widow Craigie had died, and Fanny's father, the wealthy Nathan Appleton, purchased Craigie House for the newlyweds.[3]

Figure 3.3. Photograph of horse-drawn carriages on Beacon Street, Boston, circa 1880s. This is the street where Fanny Appleton lived before she married Henry. Courtesy Boston Public Library, Print Department.

For the next eleven years, Henry continued with his teaching duties at Harvard, finding time when he could for his own writing. During this period, he published the long poem "Evangeline." He also published *The Poets and Poetry of Europe.* Fanny wrote the introduction to this book and helped him proofread it because Henry suffered from distressing eye trouble.[4]

Henry and Fanny loved each other and their children dearly. He wrote a poem in 1859 called "The Children's Hour" mentioning his three daughters, "grave Alice, and laughing Allegra and Edith with the golden hair." The poem became so famous that a painting of Henry's three daughters by the artist Thomas Buchanan Read was reproduced again and again in books and magazines.[5]

Figure 3.4. Painting of Henry's three daughters by Thomas Buchanan Read in 1859. At the top is Alice, to the right is Anne Allegra, called "Annie," and Edith is to the left. Courtesy National Park Service, Longfellow House–Washington's Headquarters National Historic Site.

"The Children's Hour"

Between the dark and the daylight,
    When the night is beginning to lower,
Comes a pause in the day's occupations,
    That is known as the Children's Hour.

I hear in the chamber above me
    The patter of little feet,
The sound of a door that is opened,
    And voices soft and sweet.

From my study I see in the lamplight,
    Descending the broad hall stair
Grave Alice, and laughing Allegra,
    And Edith with golden hair.

A whisper and then a silence:
    Yet I know by their merry eyes
They are plotting and planning together
    To take me by surprise.

A sudden rush from the stairway,
    A sudden raid from the hall!
By three doors left unguarded
    They enter my castle wall!

They climb up into my turret
    O'er the arms and back of my chair;
If I try to escape, they surround me;
    They seem to be everywhere.

They almost devour me with kisses,
    Their arms about me entwine,
Till I think of the Bishop of Bingen
    In his Mouse-Tower on the Rhine!

Do you think, O blue-eyed banditti,
    Because you have scaled the wall,
Such an old mustache as I am
    Is not a match for you all!

I have you fast in my fortress,
    And will not let you depart,
But put you down into the dungeon
    In the round-tower of my heart.

And there will I keep you forever,
    Yes, forever and a day,
Till the walls shall crumble to ruin,
    And moulder in dust away![6]

Malden, Mass.
Feb. 22. 1882

Dear Mr. Longfellow.

I am only a little girl, 12 years old, but I have read some of your poems and I love you very much. I suppose a great many distinguished men will send you presents for your birthday but I can only send you my good wishes and hope you will have a great many more happy birthdays. I go to the Centre School and we are going to have rhetoricals on your birthday at which I am going to recite your "Children's Hour." I hope I haven't annoyed you by writing but I wanted to so much and mama said she didn't think it was wrong.

I send you a kiss and hope you will have a happy birthday.

Yours lovingly,
Alice E. Wilde

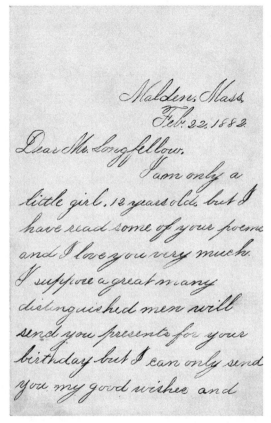

Figure 3.5. Photograph of Alice E. Wilde's letter, page 1. [bMS Am 1340.7 Houghton Library, Harvard University.]

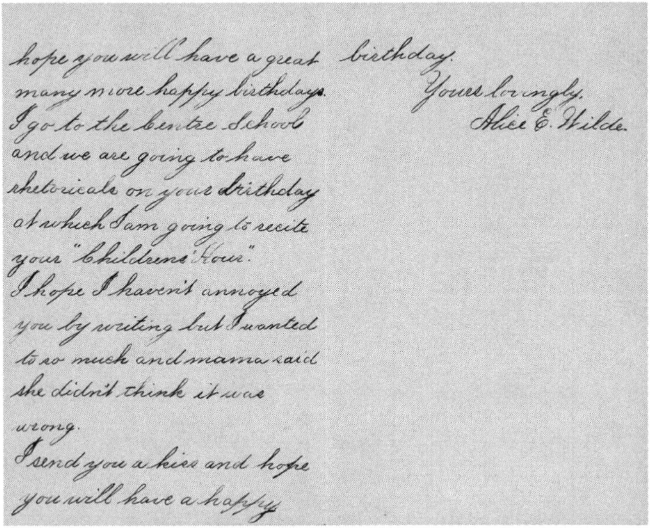

hope you will have a great many more happy birthdays. I go to the Centre School and we are going to have rhetoricals on your birthday at which I am going to recite your "Childrens Hour". I hope I haven't annoyed you by writing but I wanted to so much and mama said she didn't think it was wrong.

I send you a kiss and hope you will have a happy birthday.

Yours lovingly,

Alice E. Wilde.

Figure 3.6. Photograph of Alice E. Wilde's letter, page 2. [bMS Am 1340.7 Houghton Library, Harvard University.]

Henry and Fanny also had two sons, Charley and Ernest. He wrote a poem for each of them. The poem for Ernest was called "The Castle-Builder," and the one for Charley was called "Verses to a Child."[7] One daughter, named Fanny for her mother, died in

1848 when she was seventeen months old. Henry and Fanny were terribly distraught by her death. Henry wrote a poem about her called "Resignation."[8]

Fanny was a warm, doting, imaginative mother who was concerned about the spiritual and moral development of her children. Here is part of a story she recorded in her journal on January 14, 1849. She told it to Charley and Ernest when they were very young.

Told them story of the little boy (my version of Jack and the Beanstalk) who planted [a] bean in the garden and it began to grow, and every time he did a good thing it shot up higher, and when he was generous and kind a beautiful flower bloomed on it, and when he was naughty the flower died, and it grew shorter again, and the leaves turned black and dropped off. And so it grew up and up to the sky, and he found he could climb up it, putting his feet on the leaves as steps, and when he reached the top the last flowers sprang to his shoulders and made little wings with which he flew among the clouds till he reached a lovely garden, where all good children lived and flew about.[9]

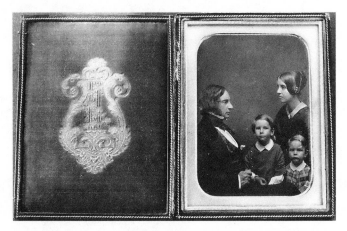

Figure 3.7. Fanny, Henry, Charley, and Ernest in 1849, from a daguerreotype (LONG 4807). Ernest is on the right and Charley is on the left. Courtesy National Park Service, Longfellow House–Washington's Headquarters National Historic Site.

That same year, Henry wrote his poem called "Children."

"Children"

Come to me, O ye children!
 For I hear you at your play,
And the questions that perplexed me
 Have vanished quite away.

Ye open wide the eastern windows
 That look towards the sun,
Where thoughts are singing swallows
 And the brooks of morning run.

In your hearts are the birds and the sunshine,
 In your thoughts the brooklet's flow,
But mine is the wind of Autumn
 And the first fall of the snow.

Ah! What would the world be to us
 If the children were no more?
We should dread the desert behind us
 Worse than the dark before.

What the leaves are to the forest,
With light and air for food,
Ere their sweet and tender juices
Have been hardened into wood,—

That to the world are children;
Through them it feels the glow
Of a brighter and sunnier climate
Than reaches the trunks below.

Come to me, O ye children!
And whisper in my ear
What the birds and the winds are singing
In your sunny atmosphere.

For what of all our contrivings,
And the wisdom of our books,
When compared with your caresses,
And the gladness of your looks?

Ye are better than all the ballads
That ever were sung or said;
For ye are living poems,
And all the rest are dead.[10]

But all was not so bright and sunny. The country was terribly divided on the issue of slavery between the Northern or free states and the Southern or slaveholding states. Slaves were black people who were forcibly taken from their homes in Africa and shipped to America to become the property of white owners in the Southern states. They had no rights and could be bought, sold, or whipped at their owner's whim. They were forced to work very hard, picking cotton or tobacco, splitting logs, cooking, and cleaning, as well as many other tasks. It was against the law for anyone to teach a slave how to read and write.

Slaves could be truly free if they escaped up North all the way to Canada, but it was very dangerous for them to run away. If they were caught, they could be beaten or even killed. In order to escape, slaves traveled mostly by foot on the Underground Railroad, a network of secret hideouts or "stations" from the slaveholding South to the free North. The "stations" were homes or businesses of free blacks, Quakers, and others who were willing to hide slaves until they could make their way to another "station" on their way up

North. The Fugitive Slave Law of 1850 specified that slaves who escaped to one of the Northern states be returned to their owners in the South. Slave catchers roamed the Northern towns and cities, including Boston. Slave catchers didn't care whether or not the people they captured were escaped slaves. All black people were in danger. Henry wrote in his journal on May 29, 1858, "If anybody wants to break a law, let him break the Fugitive-Slave law. That is all it is for."[11]

Henry's best friend, Charles Sumner[12], was an abolitionist. He spoke out strongly against slavery.

Figure 3.8. Photograph of Henry *(right)* with Charles Sumner *(left)* taken by Alexander Gardner in December 1863 in Washington, DC, "The Politics and Poetry of New England." Courtesy National Park Service, Longfellow House–Washington's Headquarters National Historic Site.

Henry wrote a small volume called *Poems on Slavery* that was published in 1842. Some people who read the poems and believed in slavery harshly criticized Henry. Others, like President Abraham Lincoln, appreciated his poems very much. Henry's poem "The Building of the Ship" was published in 1849. The word *ship* in the poem refers to the nation or the Union. Abraham Lincoln was so moved by it that tears came to his eyes when it was read aloud to him.[13] The poem was about the terrible divisions that the country was experiencing. Perhaps these lines touched Lincoln the most:

> **Sail on, O UNION, strong and great!**
> **Humanity with all its fears,**
> **With all the hopes of future years,**
> **Is hanging breathless on thy fate![14]**

At that time, the schools in Boston were segregated. Black children and white children weren't allowed to go to school together. Fanny wrote in December 1849 to her brother, Tom:

Sumner has been vindicating in court the rights of a little black girl against the city of Boston for free admission to the free school, to be able to go like white children to the one nearest her home, and not forced to traverse the town to an African school.[15]

The five-year-old girl was Sarah Roberts. Her father had enlisted the help of attorney Charles Sumner in his legal fight against segregation. The case was brought to the Massachusetts Supreme Court, but Sumner lost. In 1855, however, there was a law passed in the Massachusetts legislature that said the Boston schools must be integrated—black children and white children were to attend school together.[16] Schools in Cambridge, as in the rest of the state, were not segregated.

Figure 3.9. Picture of Craigie House, watercolor and pencil, undated and unsigned. Henry probably made it in the 1850s with the help of one of his children. Courtesy National Park Service, Longfellow House–Washington's Headquarters National Historic Site.

Chapter 4

*"Which of your poems
do you think is written the best?"*

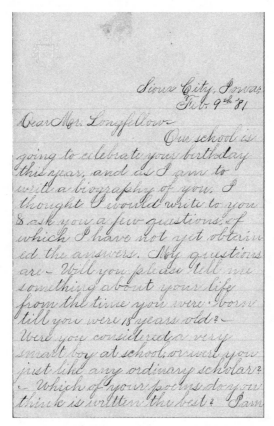

Figure 4.1. Photograph of Helen E. Hoskins's letter, page 1. [bMS Am 1340.7 Houghton Library, Harvard University.]

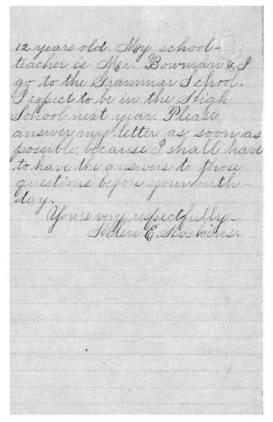

Figure 4.2. Photograph of Helen E. Hoskins's letter, page 2. [bMS Am 1340.7 Houghton Library, Harvard University.]

Sioux City, Iowa;
Feb. 9th '81

Dear Mr. Longfellow~

> *Our school is going to celebrate your birthday this year, and as I am to write a biography of you, I thought I would write to you & ask you a few questions of which I have not yet obtained the answers. My questions are—Will you please tell me something about your life from the time you were born till you were 18 years old?—Were you considered a very smart boy at school; or were you just like any ordinary scholar?—Which of your poems do you think is written the best? I am 12 years old. My school-teacher is Mr. Bowman & I go to the Grammar School. I expect to be in the High School next year. Please answer my letter as soon as possible because I shall have to have the answers to those questions before your birthday.*
> *Yours very respectfully—*
> *Helen E. Hoskins.*

*I*n his journals, Henry expressed his constant struggle with his duties as a professor, his waiting correspondence, and his desire to write poetry. He wrote in his journal on October 11, 1846:

> *I am in despair at the swift flight of time, and the utter impossibility I feel to lay upon anything permanent. All my hours and days go to perishable things. College takes half the time; and other people, with their interminable letters and poems and requests and demands, take the rest. I have hardly a moment to think of my own writings, and am cheated of some of life's fairest hours.*[1]

In 1854, when Henry was forty-seven years old, he retired from Harvard College in order to write full time. That year, he began writing a long poem based upon his research called "The Song of Hiawatha," about the life and lore of Native Americans. The poem was published in 1855 and was very well received by the public. Children enjoyed reciting it. Here are a few verses from the introduction.

Should you ask me, whence these stories?
Whence these legends and traditions,
With the odors of the forest,
With the dew and damp of meadows,
With the curling smoke of wigwams,
With the rushing of great rivers,
With their frequent repetitions,
And their wild reverberations,
As of thunder in the mountains?
 I should answer, I should tell you,
 "From the forests and the prairies,
 From the great lakes of the Northland,
 From the land of the Ojibways,
 From the land of the Dacotahs,
 From the mountains, moors and fenlands
 Where the heron, the Shuh-shuh-gah,
 Feeds among the reeds and rushes.
 I repeat them as I heard them
 From the lips of Nawadaha,
 The musician, the sweet singer . . ."[2]

Wallingford, Feb. 7th 1880.

Dear Sir,

We have been celebrating your birthday in three departments of the Wallingford, Graded, School. In the department in which I attend they recited several selections from your writings, they recited Hiawatha; The Village Blacksmith, and several others. I recited Picture Writing, where Hiawatha taught his people. I enjoyed it very much. I wish you could have been here and heard us. As I am only thirteen years old you will not expect me to write a very long letter, so I will close.—

Yours, respectfully.
Robert Bolton.
Wallingford.
P.O. box 135.   Conn. [Connecticut]

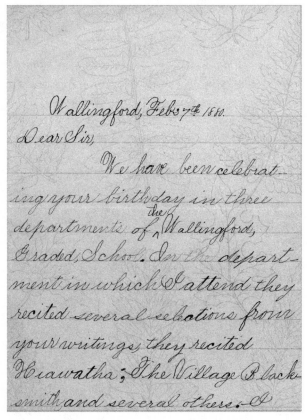

Wallingford, Feb. 7th 1880.

Dear Sir,

We have been celebrat-
ing your birthday in three
departments of the Wallingford,
Graded, School. In the depart-
ment in which I attend they
recited several selections from
your writings; they recited
Hiawatha; The Village Black-
smith and several others. I

Figure 4.3. Photograph of Robert Bolton's letter, page 1. [bMS Am 1340.7 Houghton Library, Harvard University.]

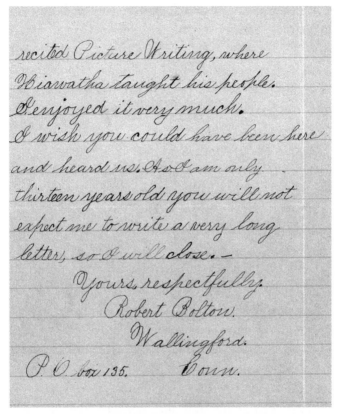

recited Picture Writing, where Hiawatha taught his people. I enjoyed it very much. I wish you could have been here and heard us. As I am only thirteen years old you will not expect me to write a very long letter, so I will close. —

Yours, respectfully,
Robert Bolton.
Wallingford.
P. O. box 135.   Conn.

Figure 4.4. Photograph of Robert Bolton's letter, page 2. [bMS Am 1340.7 Houghton Library, Harvard University.]

Henry wrote in pencil standing up at a desk in his study near one of the windows that overlooked the Charles River.[3] The morning hours were easiest on his eyes.[4] Sometimes, his writing was interrupted by spontaneous visits from his children. His daughter Alice remembered that in Henry's study "in a drawer of one of the bookcases was a collection of little pictures drawn by my father in pencil, which he used with great facility, 'The Wonderful Adventures of Peter Piper.' These were a constant source of delight, as new adventures would suddenly appear from time to time, and we never knew what the wonderful Peter Piper would do next."[5]

Henry liked spending quiet evenings at home with Fanny, who often read aloud to him. He enjoyed dining with his friends and smoking his cigars.[6] Henry had a velvet maroon smoking jacket.[7] He especially enjoyed meeting with his friends at a Boston hotel called the Parker House. They would eat lunch and visit for hours on the last Saturday of every month except during the summertime. They called their meetings the Saturday Club.[8] At another club, named the Atlantic Club, Henry and some of these same friends started a magazine in 1857 called the *Atlantic Monthly*. Two of the famous friends who gathered through the years of 1855–1870 were Oliver Wendell Holmes, a doctor and writer, and John Greenleaf Whittier, a poet.[9] Years later, in the 1880s, the portraits of Henry and these famous American writers and friends hung from the schoolroom walls side by side.

One famous friend who came to visit him from London was the writer Charles Dickens.[10] Another famous friend was the writer Nathaniel Hawthorne, who had gone to Bowdoin College at the same time as Henry.[11] Henry made friends with actors and singers too. He loved to attend the opera and the theater whenever he could. Sometimes he and Fanny attended performances of his own poems![12]

Henry and Fanny also attended formal dances or balls. Henry liked to dress up in his frock coat, top hat, and cane, while Fanny had some very fancy evening dresses. One dress was yellow with black lace ruffles and another was lavender with beige lace.[13]

Figure 4.5. Photograph of Henry with hat and cane, circa 1858. Courtesy National Park Service, Longfellow House—Washington's Headquarters National Historic Site.

Figure 4.6. Picture of Fanny in 1859 from a drawing by Samuel Worcester Rowse. Courtesy National Park Service, Longfellow House–Washington's Headquarters National Historic Site.

In the summer, Henry and his family went to their cottage in Nahant, Massachusetts, near the sea. They had a coachman and a carriage and enjoyed rides along the beach.[14] Fanny wrote in a letter to her sister-in-law Mary:

> *The children are very happy here, as you can imagine. Charley and Erny [Ernest] have a boat, and are out from daybreak fishing and paddling about, but the latter often comes home to play fairy-land with Alice upon the rocks, collecting sea-weed and shells and arranging them in crevices. Even little Edy [Edith] joins in this fun.*[15]

Back at Craigie House, the Longfellows had servants who worked for them. Some lived on the third floor of their big house.[16]

Henry made friends with all kinds of people, not just those who were rich or famous. His daughter Alice wrote that he treated everyone with respect.

His house was known to all the vagrant trains, and to all he was equally genial and kind. There was no change of voice or manner in talking with the humblest member of society; and I am inclined to think the friendly chat in Italian with the organ-grinder and the little old woman-peddlar, or the discussions with the old Irish gardener, were quite as full of pleasure as more important conversations with travelers from Europe.[17]

Henry enjoyed the company of his children and was troubled when they were sad or sick.[18] According to Alice, in his journals, Henry noted "a walk to Fresh Pond, a shopping expedition to Boston, an afternoon building a snow-house."[19] He wrote his children affectionate letters. One letter to ten-year-old "Dearest Alice" on July 26, 1860, said "We are just starting for Stockbridge; so I must give you a kiss and say farewell till Saturday. Papa."[20]

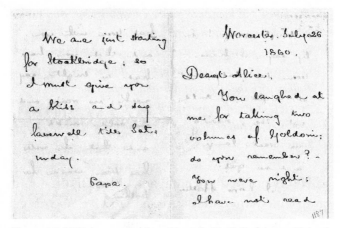

Figure 4.7. HWL letter to daughter Alice, July 26, 1860. Courtesy National Park Service, Longfellow House–Washington's Headquarters National Historic Site.

Life went along happily for Henry and his family in the shadow of the Civil War.

There was a porch that encircled Craigie House, and in the back was a beautiful garden he had designed. He loved to walk amongst the flowers and smell their fragrance.

On May 20, 1861, Henry wrote in his journal, "First grand display of buttercups in the grass. How beautiful they are! The purple buds of the lilacs tip the hedges; and the flowery tide of spring sweeps on. Everywhere in the air the warlike rumor of drums mingles discordantly with the song of birds."[21]

Henry didn't know it, but less than two months later he would experience the most horrible tragedy of his life.

Chapter 5

"It was my cat's birthday yesterday."

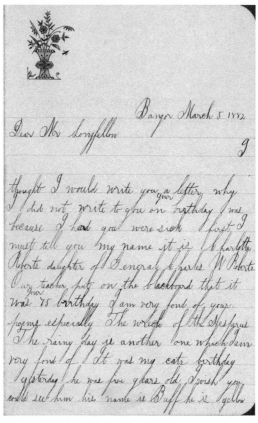

Figure 5.1. Photograph of Charlotte Roberts's letter, page 1.
[bMS Am 1340.7 Houghton Library, Harvard University.]

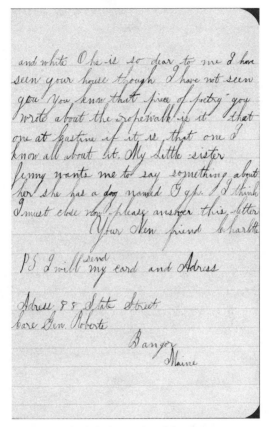

and white. O he is so dear to me I have
seen your house though I have not seen
you You know that piece of poetry you
wrote about the ropewalk is it that
one at Castine if it is, that one I
know all about it. My little sister
Jenny wants me to say something about
her she has a dog named Gyp. I think
I must close now please answer this letter
                    Your New friend Charltte

P S I will send my card and Adress

Adress 88 State Street
care Gen. Roberts
                    Bangor
                        Maine

Figure 5.2. Photograph of Charlotte Roberts's letter, page 2.
[bMS Am 1340.7 Houghton Library, Harvard University.]

Bangor March 5 1882

Dear Mr Longfellow

I thought I would write you a letter why I did not write to you on your birthday was because I heard you were sick first I must tell you my name it is Charlotte Roberts daughter of General Charles W Roberts Our teacher put on the blackboard that it was your 75 birthday I am very fond of your poems especially The wreck of the Hesperus The rainy day is another one which I am very fond of. It was my cat's birthday yesterday he was five years old I wish you could see him his name is Buff he is yellow and white O he is so dear to me I have seen your house though I have not seen you You know that piece of poetry you wrote about the ropewalk is it that one at Castine if it is that one I know all about it. My little sister Jenny wants me to say something about her she has a dog named Gyp. I think I must close now please answer this letter

Your New friend Charlotte

PS I will send my card and Adress

Adress 88 State Street
Care Gen. Roberts

Bangor
Maine

*O*n July 9, 1861, it was so warm that Fanny, sitting in the library of the house, decided to cut locks of Edith's and Annie's hair and send them to relatives. Hair was snipped and a match was struck to light a candle to seal the wax on the envelope. Suddenly, the match brushed against Fanny's dress and set it on fire!

Henry was resting in his study when the screams startled him and he rushed into the library. He wrapped a rug around his wife, trying to smother the flames. In the process, his face and his hands were badly burned. A doctor was sent for, but Fanny died the next day. Henry was in too much pain, physically and emotionally, to go to the funeral, which took place in the library of Craigie House.[1] Henry's love for his wife had been so deep that he wrote to her sister, Mary, on August 18, 1861, "I never looked at her without a thrill of pleasure; she never came into a room where I was without my heart beating quicker, nor went out without my feeling that something of the light went with her. I loved her so entirely, and

I know she was very happy."[2] Toward the end of his life he wrote a poem about her called "The Cross of Snow."[3]

Henry's face and neck were so badly burned that he couldn't shave, and so he grew a beard that soon turned from brown to white. This is how children in classrooms across America came to know him as they looked up at his portrait hanging upon their walls.

After Fanny's death, Henry hired an English governess, Miss Hannah Davie, who taught the youngest children, eight-year-old Edith and six-year-old Annie. Along with a group of six neighborhood children, they used the room above Henry's study as their schoolroom. They studied arithmetic, history, science, Latin, dictation, spelling, definitions, reading, and compositions.[4] They even created their own magazine they called *The Secret*, and included in it stories and drawings.[5] Before school, the children played tag and I spy.[6] In the winter, they loved to go sledding down the hill in the front yard of Craigie House. Henry never once told them to be quiet, even though they played right near his study![7]

Henry's daughter Alice recalled that her family had "a succession of pets: dogs, rabbits, hens, and turtles in a tub in the garden. A Scotch terrier, named 'Trap,' was a most important member of the family for twelve years, a constant companion of my father."[8]

One of the stories in *The Secret* was called "The Insult" and featured the family dog, Trap. It was written by Henry's daughter, Annie, when she was ten years old.[9]

The Insult

As Trap Longfellow was going down street the other day, he met a little girl coming up with her father. The little girl said "Oh papa! what an ugly dog!" The Papa answered "Why ugly, my dear? he seems to be a very good little dog" "Yes" said the little girl, "but he has got a body just like a pig!" Poor Trap!

Figure 5.3. Photograph of Henry with Trap, circa 1864. Courtesy National Park Service, Longfellow House–Washington's Headquarters National Historic Site.

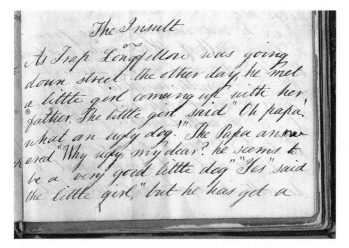

The Insult

As Trap Longfellow was going down street the other day, he met a little girl comeing up with her father. The little girl said "Oh papa, what an ugly dog!'" The Papa answered "Why ugly my dear? he seems to be a very good little dog" "Yes" said the little girl, "but he has got a

Figure 5.4. Photograph of "The Insult," page 1. *THE SECRET*, vol. 2, June 1865. Courtesy National Park Service, Longfellow House–Washington's Headquarters National Historic Site.

12   *The Secret*

body just like a pig!" Poor Trap!

Figure 5.5. Photograph of "The Insult," page 2. *THE SECRET*, vol. 2, June 1865. Courtesy National Park Service, Longfellow House–Washington's Headquarters National Historic Site.

After Fanny died, Henry was so sad that for a long time he could not write. He turned to translating Dante's *The Divine Comedy* from the Italian into English, and this seemed to comfort him. On Wednesday evenings, he gathered a few of his friends around him and shared his translation with them as it progressed, calling these get-togethers "The Dante Club."[10] He also continued with his annual visits to Portland. The flowers in the garden were soothing to gaze upon, as was the face of his dear sister Anne. Anne's husband, George Pierce, had died suddenly after only three years of marriage, and Anne had returned to the Portland house to live.

Henry's publisher and friend, James T. Fields, went with him for a ride one day to the Red Horse Tavern in Sudbury, Massachusetts. The Red Horse Tavern had once been called the Wayside Inn.[11] Henry wrote a series of poems about a group of travelers telling stories to each other there. *Tales of the Wayside Inn* was published in 1863. His poem "Paul Revere's Ride" was part of this collection. Here are the first two verses and the last verse:

Listen, my children, and you shall hear
Of the midnight ride of Paul Revere,
On the eighteenth of April, in Seventy-five;
Hardly a man is now alive
Who remembers that famous day and year.

He said to his friend, "If the British march
By land or sea from the town to-night,
Hang a lantern aloft in the belfry arch
Of the North Church tower as a signal light,—
One, if by land, and two, if by sea;
And I on the opposite shore will be,
Ready to ride and spread the alarm
Through every Middlesex village and farm,
For the country folk to be up and to arm." . . .

So through the night rode Paul Revere;
And so through the night went his cry of alarm
To every Middlesex village and farm,—
A cry of defiance and not of fear,
A voice in the darkness, a knock at the door,
And a word that shall echo forevermore!
For, borne on the night-wind of the Past,
Through all our history, to the last,

> **In the hour of darkness and peril and need,**
> **The people will waken and listen to hear**
> **The hurrying hoof-beats of that steed,**
> **And the midnight message of Paul Revere.**[12]

The poem became so famous that to the present day, it has become the way many people think things really happened when, in fact, Henry used his imagination about some of the details.[13] Henry's lines "Hang a lantern aloft in the belfry arch / Of the North Church tower as a signal light,— / One, if by land, and two, if by sea / And I on the opposite shore will be" imply that Paul Revere was waiting and watching to count the lanterns used, when, in fact, he knew the British troops were traveling by sea. Henry also made no mention of another rider that night for the Sons of Liberty—William Dawes.[14]

Oil City, Pa., [Pennsylvania] Feb. 28th, 1881

Mr. H. W. Longfellow,—

Dear Sir:

I will write you a short letter this afternoon. I am in the A class Primary room A. My teachers name is Mifs C. A. Wilson. We celebrated your birthday today as yesterday was Sabbath. The poems that we recited were, The Wreck of the Hesperus, The Children's Hour, The Builders, The Bridge, Killed at the Ford, The Day is Done, The Village Blacksmith, The Rainy Day, Twilight and I spoke Paul Revere's ride. We had thirty visitors. We had drawings and number-work on the black-board. While I was committing my piece my little brother, Marcellus, (papa calls him his little General, as he is three years old) learned nearly all of Paul Revere's ride. I have only to tell him now and then a word. I have all your poems, as my own. I think they are very nice. I am eight years old. Enclosed find my picture. I would be delighted to receive yours in return. Hoping that you may live to see many happy returns of this day I remain,

Yours most sincerely,

Winifred Welles Wagner.

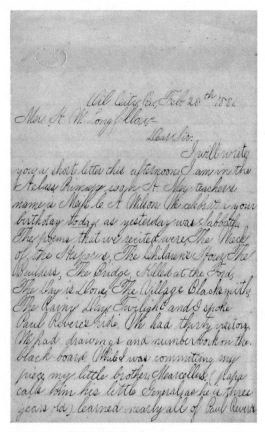

Figure 5.6. Photograph of Winifred Welles Wagner's letter, page 1.
[bMS Am 1340.7 Houghton Library, Harvard University.]

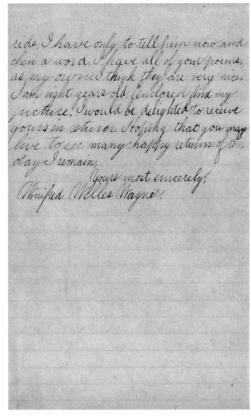

Figure 5.7. Photograph of Winifred Welles Wagner's letter, page 2.
[bMS Am 1340.7 Houghton Library, Harvard University.]

The same year *Tales of the Wayside Inn* was published, Henry's son Charley ran away from home at the age of eighteen to become a second lieutenant in the First Massachusetts Calvary during the Civil War. Henry was very worried about him! Charley became ill with camp fever or malaria and spent the summer of 1863 recuperating in Nahant.[15] A few months later, he rejoined his regiment in Virginia but was badly wounded when a bullet "shot through both shoulders."[16] Henry and Ernest met him in Alexandria, Virginia. He rested for a few days and a doctor tended to him in a hotel room before they returned home to Cambridge.[17]

Charley later traveled to India, Japan, and China, and he brought back vases and other pieces of art from these lands and other places where his father had never been. Henry's poems, however, *had* traveled to the Far East. According to his publisher, James T. Fields, Henry's poem "A Psalm of Life" was so famous that it was printed on fans in China![18] Here is the first verse:

√√ **Tell me not, in mournful numbers,**
　　　Life is but an empty dream!—
　　For the soul is dead that slumbers,
　　　And things are not what they seem.[19]

Henry had a chance to revisit some of the places he had traveled to in his youth when he spent fifteen months in Europe from June 1868 through August 1869. His brother Samuel Longfellow; his two widowed sisters, Anne Longfellow Pierce and Mary Longfellow Greenleaf; his sons, Charley and Ernest, and Ernest's new wife, Harriet Spelman Longfellow; his brother-in-law, Tom Appleton; his daughters, Alice, Edith, and Annie; and their governess, Miss Hannah Davie, all made the journey with him.[20] Ten years later, Edith would marry Richard Henry Dana III. Henry's second grandson, born in January 1881, was named for him—Henry Wadsworth Longfellow Dana. In 1885, Annie would marry Joseph Gilbert Thorp Jr. and would have five daughters. Alice and Charley would never marry.

Figure 5.8. Photograph of Henry and his family in Venice, Italy, the summer of 1869, taken by A. Sorgato. *Standing left to right*: Henry's brother Samuel; his daughter Alice; brother-in-law, Tom Appleton; Henry's son Ernest, and Ernest's new wife, Harriet Spelman Longfellow. *Seated left to right*: Henry's sister Mary Longfellow Greenleaf; Henry's daughters Edith and Annie; Henry's sister Anne Longfellow Pierce. Henry is seated at the center. Courtesy National Park Service, Longfellow House–Washington's Headquarters National Historic Site.

While in England, Henry received honorary degrees from Cambridge University and Oxford University.[21] Queen Victoria, whose name became linked with an entire period in history known as the Victorian era, invited Henry to come to Windsor Castle![22] But "no foreign tribute touched him deeper than the words of an English hod-carrier, [servant who carried bricks] who came up to the carriage door at Harrow and asked permission to take the hand of the man who had written the *Voices of the Night.*"[23]

Chapter 6

*"Our teacher read to us
the poem about the blacksmith,
and then told us about
the children of Cambridge
making you a present of a chair."*

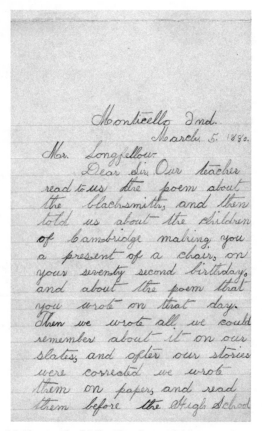

Figure 6.1. Photograph of Callie Obenchain et al. letter, page 1.
[bMS Am 1340.7 Houghton Library, Harvard University.]

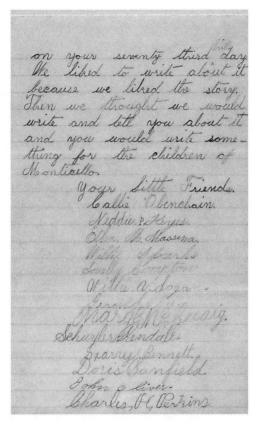

Figure 6.2. Photograph of Callie Obenchain et al. letter, page 2. [bMS Am 1340.7 Houghton Library, Harvard University.]

Monticello Ind.[Indiana]
March 5. 1880.

Mr. Longfellow,

Dear Sir. Our teacher read to us the poem about the blacksmith, and then told us about the children of Cambridge making you a present of a chair, on your seventy second birthday, and about the poem that you wrote on that day. Then we wrote all we could remember about it on our slates, and after our stories were corrected we wrote them on paper, and read them before the High School on your seventy third day. We liked to write about it because we liked the story. Then we thought we would write and tell you about it and you would write something for the children of Monticello.

Your Little Friends.
Callie Obenchain.
Neddie. P. Keyes.
Etha. M. Massena
Willie Sparks
Luelly Compton
Willie. N. Logan.
Graer Gadgee
Mary McCraig.

Schuyler Kendall.
Larry Bennett.
Dorris Banfield
John Oliver.
Charles, H, Perkins.

*I*n 1876, the "spreading chestnut tree" from Henry's poem "The Village Blacksmith" was thought to be in the way of traffic, and the Public Works Department of the City of Cambridge decided to chop it down because its branches dipped so low that horses and carriages couldn't pass by without bumping against them. Many people, however, were upset at the possibility of losing this tree that Henry had made so famous in his poem. Some adults and children protested, but it was cut down, much to their great disappointment.[1]

Henry made a sketch of the blacksmith shop and the "spreading chestnut tree" in the year 1840. Imagine how high and wide it must have grown by the year 1876!

Figure 6.3. Photograph of Henry's sketch of the chestnut tree, 1840.
Courtesy National Park Service, Longfellow House–Washington's
Headquarters National Historic Site and Alice Dana Cavette.

Henry's neighbors, Eben and Phoebe Horsford, thought it would be a wonderful idea to save some of the wood from the tree and have an armchair built out of it to give as a birthday gift to the poet. Six hundred Cambridge schoolchildren eagerly helped by donating their dimes to the project,[2] and the Horsfords contributed the rest of the money.[3] The chair was designed by William Pitt Preble Longfellow, the poet's nephew, and it was made by H. Edgar Hartwell of Boston.[4]

The chair was decorated with carvings of horse chestnut flowers and around the base was carved four lines from "The Village Blacksmith":

> **And children coming home from school**
> **Look in at the open door**
> **And catch the burning sparks that fly**
> **Like chaff from a threshing floor.**[5]

There was a brass plaque attached to the wood underneath the leather cushion. The plaque said:

To

The Author

of

The Village Blacksmith:

This chair, made from the wood

Of the Spreading Chestnut Tree

is presented as

an expression of grateful regard

and veneration

by

The Children of Cambridge:

Who with their friends join in

Best wishes and congratulations

On

This Anniversary.

February 27. 1879.[6]

Later that day, Henry turned to his journal to record these thoughts: "February 27th. My seventy-second birthday. A present from the children of Cambridge of a beautiful armchair, made from the wood of the Village Blacksmith's chestnut tree."[7]

Before the day had ended, Henry decided to give

a gift back to the children. This is the poem he wrote for them:

"From My Arm-Chair"
To the Children of Cambridge
Who presented me, on my Seventy-second Birthday,
February 27th, 1879, this chair made from the wood
Of the Village Blacksmith's Chestnut Tree

Am I king, that I should call my own
    This splendid ebon throne?
Or by what reason, or what right divine,
    Can I proclaim it mine?

Only, perhaps, by right divine of song
    It may to me belong;
Only because the spreading chestnut tree
    Of old was sung by me.

Well I remember it in all its prime,
    When in the summer-time
The affluent foliage of its branches made
    A cavern of cool shade.

There, by the blacksmith's forge, beside the street
    Its blossoms white and sweet
Enticed the bees, until it seemed alive,
    And murmured like a hive.

And when the winds of autumn, with a shout,
    Tossed its great arms about,
The shining chestnuts, bursting from the sheath,
    Dropped to the ground beneath.

And now some fragments of its branches bare,
    Shaped as a stately chair,
Have by my hearthstone found a home at last,
    And whisper of the past.

The Danish king could not in all his pride
    Repel the ocean tide,
But, seated in this chair, I can in rhyme
    Roll back the tide of Time.

I see it again, as one in vision sees,
    The blossoms and the bees,
And hear the children's voices shout and call,
    And the brown chestnuts fall.

I see the smithy with its fires aglow,
    I hear the bellows blow,
And the shrill hammers on the anvil beat
    The iron white with heat!

And thus, dear children, have ye made for me
    This day a jubilee,
And to my more than threescore years and ten
    Brought back my youth again.

The heart hath its own memory, like the mind,
    And in it are enshrined
The precious keepsakes, into which is wrought
    The giver's loving thought.

Only your love and your remembrance could
    Give life to this dead wood,
And make these branches, leafless now so long,
    Blossom again in song.[8]

Figure 6.4. Photograph of the Children's Chair given to Henry on his birthday in 1879. Courtesy National Park Service, Longfellow House–Washington's Headquarters National Historic Site.

Henry had copies of the poem printed up and kept them in a drawer of the bookcase near the chair in his study.[9] Many children came to his house to sit in the chair and get a copy of the poem. According to Thomas Wentworth Higginson, a student in Henry's French class at Harvard,[10] "the kindly bard gave orders that no child who wished to see the chair should be excluded, and the tramp of dirty little feet through the hall was for many months the despair of his housemaids."[11]

30 ½ Marshall St.,
Rochester, N.Y., Feb. 25th. 1882.

Dear Mr. Longfellow:

Do you like to receive letters from little boys? Perhaps you do not, but I love you very much, and I feel like telling you how sorry I was to hear that you were sick and how glad I was when I heard you were well again. I hope that you will be well and happy always. I have not forgotten how kindly you talked to me when I called to see you, and I am sure I shall remember your kind looks and words as long as I live. I often read your poems and I enjoy them very much. I have learned to recite "Paul Revere's Ride," "The Children's Hour" and "A Psalm of Life." I think they are beautiful. I hope you will come to Rochester sometime and make me a visit. It is a beautiful city. I think it looks some like Cambridge. It is called the "Flower City" because there are so many lovely gardens and nurseries here. The Genesee River and Falls are here, too. And only nine miles away is the beautiful Lake Ontario. I guess you would find a great deal to interest you in Rochester, so please come when you can.

My father is in Boston and he sends us the _Boston Journal_ every day. It is a nice paper and I like to read it. I get a letter from my grandpa once in a while. He wants me to go to Boston again, but I guess I cannot go this year.

When I was at your house you offered to give me a copy of your lines thanking the children of Cambridge for the beautiful chair they gave you. I told you that I had the verses, so you did not give them to me. I did have them then, but have lost them, and I would like them ever so much, and if you would please send them to me I would feel very thankful and give you a heart full of love.

Good-by! I hope much happiness may come to you on your birthday.

> *Your loving little friend,*
> *Warren B. Parker.*

P.S. I forgot to tell you that this year I am taking "Our Dumb Animals"—a little paper published in Boston by the "Society for the Prevention of Cruelty to Animals." It is full of nice stories about animals and birds.

> *W. B. P.*

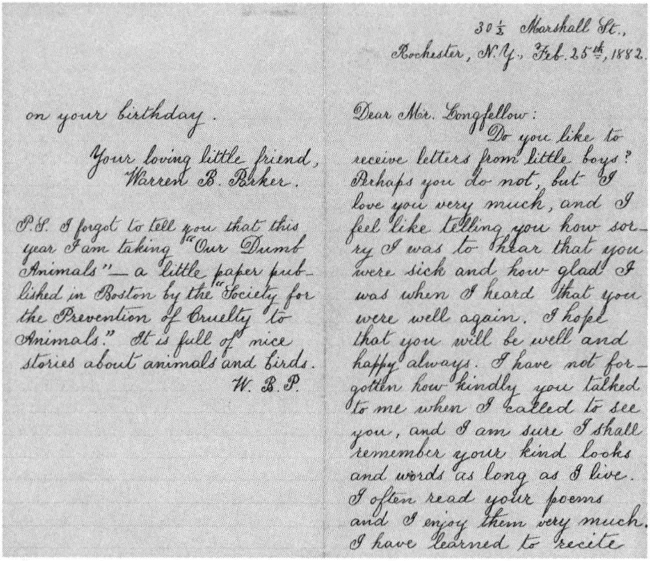

on your birthday.

Your loving little friend,
Warren B. Baker.

P.S. I forgot to tell you that this year I am taking "Our Dumb Animals"— a little paper published in Boston by the "Society for the Prevention of Cruelty to Animals." It is full of nice stories about animals and birds.
W. B. P.

30½ Marshall St.,
Rochester, N.Y., Feb. 25th, 1882.

Dear Mr. Longfellow:
Do you like to receive letters from little boys? Perhaps you do not, but I love you very much, and I feel like telling you how sorry I was to hear that you were sick and how glad I was when I heard that you were well again. I hope that you will be well and happy always. I have not forgotten how kindly you talked to me when I called to see you, and I am sure I shall remember your kind looks and words as long as I live. I often read your poems and I enjoy them very much. I have learned to recite

Figure 6.5. Photograph of Warren B. Parker's letter, page 1. [bMS Am 1340.7 Houghton Library, Harvard University.]

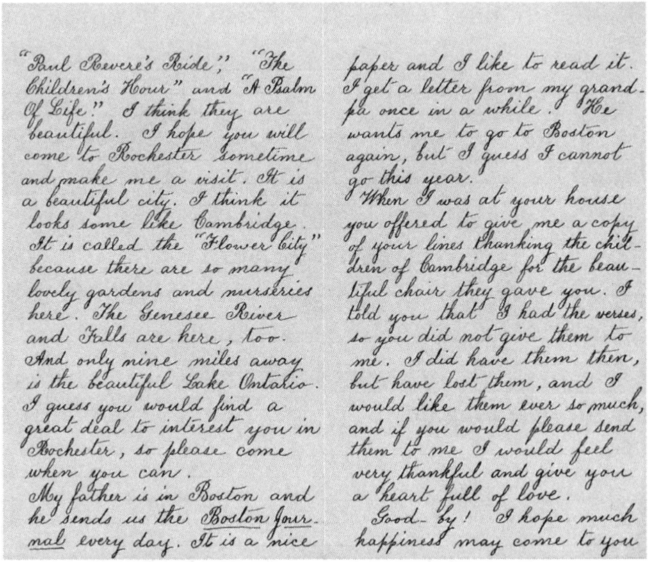

"Paul Revere's Ride," "The Children's Hour" and "A Psalm Of Life." I think they are beautiful. I hope you will come to Rochester sometime and make me a visit. It is a beautiful city. I think it looks some like Cambridge. It is called the "Flower City" because there are so many lovely gardens and nurseries here. The Genesee River and Falls are here, too. And only nine miles away is the beautiful Lake Ontario. I guess you would find a great deal to interest you in Rochester, so please come when you can.

My father is in Boston and he sends us the Boston Journal every day. It is a nice paper and I like to read it. I get a letter from my grandpa once in a while. He wants me to go to Boston again, but I guess I cannot go this year.

When I was at your house you offered to give me a copy of your lines thanking the children of Cambridge for the beautiful chair they gave you. I told you that I had the verses, so you did not give them to me. I did have them then, but have lost them, and I would like them ever so much, and if you would please send them to me I would feel very thankful and give you a heart full of love.

Good-by! I hope much happiness may come to you

Figure 6.6. Photograph of Warren B. Parker's letter, page 2. [bMS Am 1340.7 Houghton Library, Harvard University.]

Just in time for his seventy-third birthday, on February 27, 1880, Henry received a special red-and-gold book titled *The Children's Chair* from his neighbors, the Horsfords. On the inside front of the brown leather cover was the carving of the spreading chestnut tree, the blacksmith, and the children from the poem "The Village Blacksmith." Inside were the names of six hundred children who had contributed their dimes so that the special chair could be made for Henry.[12] In a letter, Phoebe Horsford apologized for the year-long delay in getting the special book to Henry.

> *My dear Mr. Longfellow.*
>
> *I am sure I owe you some apology for not having forwarded to you earlier the names of the children recorded in this little volume. Mr. Horsford's wish to bring the original color of the wood of the "spreading chestnut-tree" into the binding in some form, failed in so many instances that it has occasioned this long delay, and the book has been received only in time to ask your acceptance of it on this bright anniversary day. I hope it will be pleasant to you to find some familiar names upon the*

pages, and feel sure that the many pleasures of this day will only be increased by knowing how many children were made happy by the exquisite poem they received from you a year ago. With my most cordial regards and best wishes that this birthday may be as happy as your many friends desire to have it.

Very sincerely yours
Phoebe G. Horsford.

27 Craigie Street
February 27. 1880.[13]

Figure 6.7. Photograph of the carving of the inside cover of *The Children's Chair*. Courtesy National Park Service, Longfellow House–Washington's Headquarters National Historic Site.

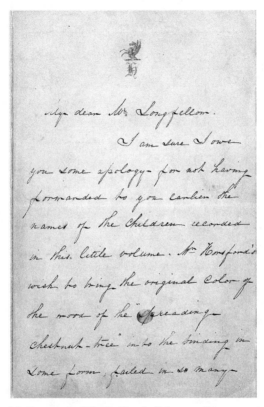

Figure 6.8. Photograph of Phoebe Horsford's letter to Henry, page 1. Courtesy National Park Service, Longfellow House–Washington's Headquarters National Historic Site.

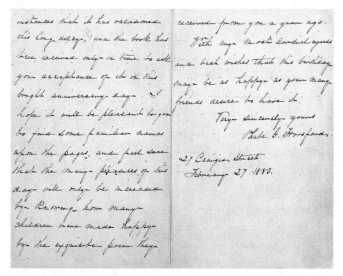

Figure 6.9. Photograph of Phoebe Horsford's letter to Henry, page 2.
Courtesy National Park Service, Longfellow House–Washington's
Headquarters National Historic Site.

Two months before Henry's seventy-fourth birthday, on December 28, 1880, Henry participated in the Children's Assembly at Harvard's Sanders Theatre to commemorate the two hundred fiftieth anniversary of the settlement of Cambridge. Over one thousand schoolchildren attended with their teachers. Many of their family members and guests of city government officials sat in the audience.[14] Henry stood upon the stage next to the special armchair[15] and said "My Dear Young Friends, . . . I am glad to see your faces and to hear your voices. I am glad to have this opportunity of thanking you in prose, as I have already done in verse for the beautiful present you made me some two years ago."[16] The mayor spoke, and then someone read aloud Henry's poem "From My Arm-Chair."[17]

Students crowded around Henry at the end of the ceremony and asked him to write his autograph in their albums, as was the custom of the day. "It was a most amusing spectacle, but the patience of the poet was inexhaustible. Over and over again, he wrote his autograph; and then, when he could write no longer, he requested that all who had not received his signature to come to his home, and he would there favor them."[18]

Chapter 7

"We have a custom in our Public Schools of celebrating the birthdays of the great poets of the day."

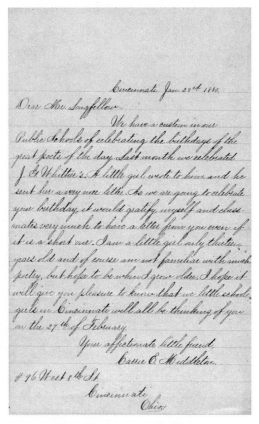

Cincinnati, Jan. 28th, 1880.

Dear Mr. Longfellow—

We have a custom in our Public Schools of celebrating the birthdays of the great poets of the day. Last month we celebrated J. G. Whittier's. A little girl wrote to him and he sent her a very nice letter. As we are going to celebrate your birthday it would gratify myself and class-mates very much to have a letter from you even if it is a short one. I am a little girl only thirteen years old and of course am not familiar with much poetry, but hope to be when I grow older. I hope it will give you pleasure to know that we little school girls in Cincinnati will all be thinking of you on the 27th of February.

Your affectionate little friend,
Carrie E. Middleton.

96 West 8th St.
Cincinnati
Ohio

Figure 7.1. Photograph of Carrie E. Middleton's letter. [bMS Am 1340.7 Houghton Library, Harvard University.]

Cincinnati. Jan. 23rd, 1880.

Dear Mr. Longfellow-

      We have a custom in our Public Schools of celebrating the birthdays of the great poets of the day. Last month we celebrated J.G. Whittier's. A little girl wrote to him and he sent her a very nice letter. As we are going to celebrate your birthday it would gratify myself and classmates very much to have a letter from you even if it is a short one. I am a little girl only thirteen years old and of course am not familiar with much poetry, but hope to be when I grow older. I hope it will give you pleasure to know that we little schoolgirls in Cincinnati will all be thinking of you on the 27th of February.

      Your affectionate little friend,
      Carrie E. Middleton.

#96 West 8th St.
    Cincinnati
    Ohio

*M*r. John Bradley Peaslee, superintendent of schools in Cincinnati, started the tradition in 1880 of celebrating the birthdays of notable writers such as John Greenleaf Whittier, Oliver Wendell Holmes, and Henry Wadsworth Longfellow to inspire the children in the schools to want to read their work instead of reading books that were thought to be poorly written or immoral.[1] This tradition of holding celebrations for the great writers spread from Cincinnati all over the country. This is the reason why Henry received so many birthday greetings throughout the rest of his life.

Mr. Peaslee wrote Henry a letter asking for some words to read to the students of Cincinnati in honor of the celebration that would be held on his seventy-third birthday.[2] Henry wrote back.

Cambridge Decr 25, 1879.

My Dear Sir,

I have had the pleasure of receiving your very interesting letter, and wish it were in my power to comply with your request to send you some lines to be read on the occasion you mention.

But want of time and numerous engagements render it impossible.

I can only send you my Christmas and New Year's greeting to the grand army of your pupils; and ask you to tell them, as I am sure you have often told them before, to live up to the best that is in them; to live noble lives, as they all may, in whatever condition they may find themselves; so that their epitaph may be that of Euripides:

"This monument does not make thee famous, O Euripides, but thou makest this monument famous."

With best wishes for yourself and all your pupils in all the schools, and the hope that your labors may be crowned with perfect success, I am, my Dear Sir,

> *Yours faithfully*
> *Henry W. Longfellow[3]*

When Mr. Peaslee read aloud Henry's letter encouraging the seventeen thousand students of the Cincinnati Public Schools to lead "noble lives,"[4] thirteen-year-old Carrie E. Middleton was among them. Six days after Henry received her letter, he wrote back. Carrie wrote again to Henry on February 1 to thank him.

CAMBRIDGE, Jan 29, 1880.

Dear Miss M——:

Yes, indeed, it will be very pleasant for me to remember that the schoolgirls of Cincinnati are thinking of me on my birthday. Few things could be more pleasant, and I assure you that when the day comes I will think of you all with equal kindness. The old can understand the young, having once been young themselves. But the young cannot so well understand the old, having never themselves been old. So perhaps you will not quite understand with how much sympathy I can enter into your feelings, and particularly when you tell me you are going to celebrate my birthday. You will have your pleasure doing it, and I will have mine in thinking you are doing it. Which will be the greater pleasure? I do not know, and you do not know and nobody can tell us. We will put it all together and each one shall have an equal share. And now I must pay you a little compliment on your nice letter, and tell you how much it has pleased me. And another little compliment on your handwriting which is as neat and clear as print.

With many thanks, your old friend and new,
HENRY W. LONGFELLOW.[5]

Cincinnati. Feb. 1st 1880.

My Dear Friend Longfellow—

I received your most welcome letter yesterday and Mamma thought best for me to answer it at once, and thank you for your kindness in answering my letter so promptly. She is going to have your reply published in the Cincinnati Commercial so that all the school-children may have the benefit of it. If you ever write to me again please do not call me, "Miss Middleton" for I am only "Carrie." I shall begin to feel more interested in poetry now, and shall read yours first. You do not know how much I should like to become acquainted with you, since you have been so kind as to write to me.

All I can do is to thank you once more.
Your Affectionate little friend
Carrie E. Middleton.

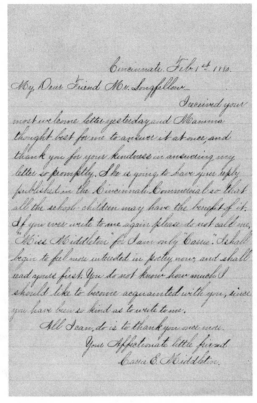

Figure 7.2. Photograph of Carrie E. Middleton's second letter to Henry.
[bMS Am 1340.7 Houghton Library, Harvard University.]

Carrie's mother, Alice M. Middleton, wrote to Henry on February 3, 1880, and thanked him for making her daughter so happy. She warned him that he would be getting many letters because his reply to Carrie was going to be published in a newspaper called the *Cincinnati Commercial*.[6]

Carrie's mother was right! Henry received a great deal of mail after his letter to Carrie was published. Henry wrote to a friend on February 7, 1880, "Perhaps you may have seen in the papers, that the Schools of Ohio are going to celebrate my birth-day. Countless letters pour in upon me from schoolboys and girls. . . . Add to all these, others from Superintendents and Teachers, and the case becomes formidable."[7] Even though Henry complained about the number of birthday letters that he received, he must have been pleased to know that he was remembered by children. Henry saved the newspaper clippings from around the country that described birthday celebrations held in his honor and put them into a special scrapbook.[8]

During the last year of his life, Henry was quite

ill. When the mayor of Portland, William Senter, invited Henry to attend a celebration of his seventy-fifth birthday, Henry wrote to him and said "My physician has prescribed absolute rest; and I do not see any chance of my being able to go to Portland in February, so slow is recovery from nervous prostration."[9]

Henry keenly felt the weight of the birthday letters upon him. In his journal entry for February 21, 1881, Henry wrote, "Some forty or more schools in the West are preparing to celebrate my seventy-fourth birthday; and all write me letters and request letters. I send to each some stanza, with signature and good wishes."[10] On February 24, Henry wrote: "Am receiving from ten to twenty letters daily with all kinds of questions and requests."[11] The next day he wrote "Letters, letters, letters! Some I answer, but many, and most, I cannot."[12]

On the back of some of the letters sent to him, Henry wrote "answered."[13] On one envelope, he wrote "Six letters from schoolgirls at Waltham."[14] According to page 1 of the *Cambridge Chronicle* for Saturday, March 5, 1881, under the heading "Old Cambridge," it said:

"—Mr. Longfellow the other day, sent this little verse to the Columbus school children, who celebrated his birthday:

If any thought of mine e'er sung or told
Has ever given delight or consolation,
Ye have repaid me back a thousand-fold
By every friendly sign and salutation."[15]

In November 1881, Henry was very relieved when he had a form printed up which said: "On account of illness, Mr. Longfellow finds it impossible to answer any letters at present. He can only acknowledge their receipt, and regret his inability to do more. Cambridge, Mass."[16] By 1882, his daughter Annie took down his dictation and often signed his letters.[17]

In a letter to a friend that he dictated to Annie on March 14, 1882, ten days before his death, Henry said, "My birthday brought upon me an avalanche of letters, fifty on that day, forty-five the next day, and so on. Since the first of Feb., with Annie's assistance I have answered 350 of them and an immense mass still remains unanswered. I sometimes wish I had not taken the ground of answering any, but that seemed to me too uncivil."[18]

The *Cambridge Chronicle* noted his birthday on page 2 with a long list of birthday celebrations for him in Cambridge and in Portland.[19] That year, on his seventy-fifth birthday, Henry must have felt overwhelmed by the letters and flowers he received and the visitors who arrived at his house.[20]

On March 11, 1882, Henry received a poem in the mail, titled "Longfellow's Seventy-Fifth Birthday," written by ten-year-old Bessie Mifflin from Columbia, Pennsylvania. George B. Mifflin, Bessie's father, enclosed the clipping of the poem that had been published in the local newspaper and a letter asking Henry to write to his daughter. Five days later, Henry wrote to Bessie Mifflin.

"Longfellow's Seventy-Fifth Birthday"

'Twas on this day long years ago,
A little boy first saw the light;
The birds, with music sweet and low,
Did welcome him with wild delight . . .

And when he sailed to foreign lands
His happy songs had gone before;
All people gave him hearts and hands,
And welcomed him from door to door.

And now we honor him to-day
The poet in his dear old home.
And though he now is old, I pray
That he may sing long years to come.[21]

Columbia, Pa. March 11. 1882.

H. W. Longfellow,

Dear Sir,

 The enclosed verses were written by my little daughter, at the request of her teacher, on the occasion of your seventy-fifth birth-day. The verses are in a measure crude, but considering the child's age we thought them very [?] indeed. Her teacher assures me that she gave her no assistance whatever. After the exercises of the day were over it was suggested to mail you a copy of her poem but little Bessie herself objected, saying that she thought it would show better taste, and be decidedly more delicate not to bore you with this amid similar little productions. However her real love for such of your poems as she is old enough to appreciate has forced her to relent, and she hesitatingly asked me to enclose you a copy of what she had written. Will you kindly draft a line to her acknowledging the receipt of the enclosed piece. The child is scarcely more than ten years old.

Very Respectfully~
Geo. B. Mifflin

P.S. I do not think she will be spoiled by this recognition on your part of her verses, as she possesses a large measure of good sense.

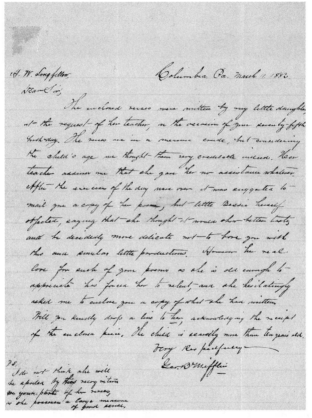

Figure 7.3. Photograph of George Mifflin's letter to Henry. [bMS Am 1340.7 Houghton Library, Harvard University.]

159

March 16, 1882.

My Dear Miss Bessie,—

I thank you very much for the poem you wrote me on my birthday, a copy of which your father sent me. It was very sweet and simple, and does you great credit. I do not think there are many girls of your age who can write so well. I myself do not know of any. It was very good of you to remember my birthday at all, and to have you remember it in so sweet a way is very pleasant and gratifying to me.[22]

Two days later, on Saturday, March 18, four schoolboys from Boston came to visit Henry. He welcomed them warmly into his study, where he wrote his name in their albums.[23] Later, he walked on his porch for exercise, though the air was quite chilly.[24] He ate dinner with a friend and said he would go to bed early because he wasn't feeling well. That night, he was in terrible pain but didn't want to wake anyone. The doctor came in the morning and diagnosed his condition as peritonitis—swelling of the abdomen. He gave him some medication to ease his suffering.[25] During the next few days, children whispered as they passed by the Longfellow House because they heard he was so sick.[26] Henry never recovered, and on Friday afternoon, March 24, he died. The bells of Cambridge tolled seventy-five times, one stroke for each year of his life.[27] "From the hour of his death to the burial, the city flags were displayed at half-mast, and the public buildings and many private dwellings were draped with emblems of mourning."[28]

The *Cambridge Chronicle* of March 25, 1882 proclaimed this headline:

> *Longfellow, Dead. It comes with a great shock to Cambridge people to learn that their chief citizen, their best-beloved, is dead.*[29]

That Sunday, he was buried in Mount Auburn Cemetery in Cambridge where his first wife, Mary; little daughter, Fanny; and beloved second wife, Fanny, were already buried. Later that afternoon, there was a public memorial service in the Harvard College chapel. Every seat was filled—people were standing wherever there was space, and many couldn't get into the building at all.[30]

Superintendent John Bradley Peaslee recorded the great sadness that his students felt upon learning of Henry's death. "The poet Longfellow was looked upon by the pupils of the Public Schools of Cincinnati not only as a great and noble writer, but as a dear old friend, whom they fondly loved. His death cast a deep gloom over the Schools. All, even the little children in the Primary grades, were affected by it."[31]

After Henry's death, his birthday continued to be celebrated in schools along with other famous American writers.[32] Almost ten years after his death, in a sketch of his life in the *Longfellow Leaflet*, the opening lines were, "A visitor to Cambridge, in Massachusetts, is very sure to make his first question, Where is the Longfellow house? and any one whom he meets will be able to tell him."[33] The Longfellow House was featured on many postcards that people sent to their relatives and friends.[34]

Henry was honored with statues and memorials. In London, England, Henry's bust, sculpted by Thomas Brock, was unveiled on March 2, 1884, in Westminster Abbey, Poets' Corner, where it still stands. Henry was the only American poet ever to have been granted such an honor.[35]

On September 29, 1888, a statue of Henry sculpted by Franklin Simmons was unveiled in Longfellow Square, Portland. [36] At the base of the statue, inside a sealed copper box, were written the names of schoolchildren from all over New England who contributed their dimes so that the statue could be built.[37] Each child who contributed received a certificate with verses from the poem "My Lost Youth" and a portrait of Henry.[38]

Figure 7.4. Photograph of the statue of Longfellow by Charles Wheeler, undated. Collections of Maine Historical Society. MMN #1132.

Henry's one-hundredth birthday in 1907 was observed with great fanfare in Cambridge. Henry's daughter Alice welcomed visitors to Craigie House from noon until 4:00 p.m. on February 27. Four hundred advance tickets were given out at the Cambridge Public Library, and when Alice realized there was such a demand for them, she allowed another four hundred tickets to be handed out that day! At the Cambridge Public Library, there was a special exhibition of the first editions of Henry's books, some of his notebooks, and portraits of him. The exhibit was open every day from February 25 through March 5, and over two thousand people came to see it.[39] Meanwhile, at Sanders Theatre, a chorus of schoolchildren sang a cantata of "The Village Blacksmith." During the celebration, teachers read aloud the same speech that Henry had presented on the stage of Sanders Theatre to schoolchildren twenty-five years ago, as part of the two hundred fiftieth anniversary of the settlement of Cambridge.[40] According to the *Boston Journal* of February 28, 1907, "So vast was the crowd at Sanders Theatre that fully half of those who went there were unable to obtain admission, and sorrowfully went away. Among these were many children, and into their eyes crept tears because they could not get inside with the others."[41]

Two years later, Henry was honored nationally. On May 7, 1909, the Henry Wadsworth Longfellow Memorial Statue, sculpted by William Cooper, was unveiled in Washington, DC, at the intersection of Connecticut and Rhode Island Avenues. Contributions came from all over the country.[42]

The Longfellow Memorial Association was formed the year that he died. Henry's children donated a strip of land in front of the house, toward the Charles River, for the memorial to be built. Thousands of school-children from across the country became members of the association when they contributed their dimes. They received a picture of his Cambridge home, while their parents became honorary members if they contributed one dollar. Famous authors who had been Henry's friends, such as Oliver Wendell Holmes, Julia Ward Howe, Mark Twain, Thomas Wentworth Higginson, and James Russell Lowell, gave readings of their work to raise money for the memorial.[43]

On October 29, 1914, the Longfellow Memorial Monument, sculpted by Daniel Chester French, was unveiled by Priscilla Thorp, Henry's granddaughter. Henry's bust stands in front of a sculptural panel depicting characters made famous in his poems, including "The Village Blacksmith."[44]

Figure 7.5. Photograph of the Longfellow Memorial Monument. Courtesy National Park Service, Longfellow House–Washington's Headquarters National Historic Site.

In 1940, Henry was honored by the United States Postal Service with a one-cent stamp showing his portrait. In a single day, thousands of these stamps were sold in Portland. The Poets Series was issued during the month of February. Henry's friend, John Greenleaf Whittier, appeared on a two-cent stamp, and his friend James Russell Lowell appeared on a three-cent stamp.[45]

In the mid-1900s, over one hundred schools across America were named for Henry. At the Longfellow School in Cambridge, now closed, it became the custom for eighth graders to hold their graduation ceremony on the east porch of the Longfellow House.[46]

Henry's daughter Alice lived in the house until her death in 1928. Henry's grandson Henry Wadsworth Longfellow Dana, called Harry, lived there until 1950. Today it is called the Longfellow House–Washington's Headquarters National Historic Site, open to the public from the end of May until the end of October, although special programs such as lectures, school visits, and concerts on the lawn take place throughout the year. Approximately forty thousand people visit the house and grounds annually.[47]

The house was closed from 1998 until 2002 so that heating and security systems, as well as a climate-controlled storage area for the archival collection, could be installed. During this time, interpreters from the house visited Cambridge classrooms to talk about Henry's life, encouraged students to write their own poetry, and even invited them to practice writing with a quill pen!

When the house reopened, renovations to the exterior included the repair of the West Porch, the roof, the front fence, and the gate. The entire house was painted, including the window shutters; and the garden was restored to the early twentieth century, the way it looked when Alice Longfellow, Henry's oldest daughter, lived at the house.[48]

Figure 7.6. Photograph of Longfellow House–Washington's Headquarters National Historic Site. Courtesy National Park Service, Longfellow House– Washington's Headquarters National Historic Site.

You can take a tour of the house, walk through Henry's study, and see the armchair that the children of Cambridge gave to him so many years ago. In 1960, the original dark green leather cushion was reupholstered to brown-black leather because it was so worn[49]—probably from so many children sitting on it! Otherwise, it is exactly the same.

Down the block, at 56 Brattle Street, is the Blacksmith House, owned and operated by the Cambridge Center for Adult Education since 1972. Built in 1808, the house once belonged to Dexter Pratt, the blacksmith who was made famous by Henry's poem "The Village Blacksmith." Pratt's blacksmith shop was just next door. On the brick wall at the side of the building, you can see a 1988 sculpture by Dimitri Gerakaris of the chestnut tree, the blacksmith's anvil, and a window, which commemorates the Window Shop, which moved to the site in 1946.[50] Look for a marker on the sidewalk to show where the "spreading chestnut tree" once stood.

Not far away is the Mount Auburn Cemetery where Henry, members of his family, and his friends, including Charles Sumner and Oliver Wendell Holmes, are buried. Every year, Henry's birthday is celebrated here. In the cemetery chapel, someone tells about Henry's life and there is a reception where birthday cake is served. The chapel celebration is followed by a walk to Henry's grave, where a wreath is placed for a special ceremony.[51]

The Wadsworth-Longfellow House in Portland was willed to the Maine Historical Society in 1901 by Anne Longfellow Pierce, Henry's sister. Today it is open to visitors from October until June and for the December holidays, and each year, about fifteen thousand people come to see it. Students from Portland and surrounding communities in grades two through five, as well as some middle-school and high-school students, travel to visit the house. You can take a tour and see Henry's flute, the kitchen hearth where the fire started in 1815, and the room where it is believed he wrote his poem "The Rainy Day."[52]

In 2001, the house was carefully restored to its 1850s interior, incorporating wallpaper and carpeting designs that Anne Longfellow Pierce and other family members referred to in their letters about the house. The window shutters were repaired, period window and door blinds were installed, walls and doors were painted, and bricks were replaced.[53] In June 2000, children from the Longfellow School in Portland raised $473 toward the renovation project.[54] Another school that contributed funds was the Longfellow Elementary School in Bozeman, Montana.[55]

Figure 7.7. Wadsworth-Longfellow House exterior photograph.
Collections of Maine Historical Society. Photograph by David Bohl, 2002.
Coll. 4016.

Every year, Henry's birthday is celebrated at the Maine Historical Society, which is the steward of his childhood home, the Wadsworth-Longfellow House. Henry's poetry is read aloud by children and adults, including the mayor and other well-known leaders in the community. In past years, Maine Historical Society staff and volunteers have appeared in costume as Henry and his sister Anne. Children are invited to illustrate Henry's poems and make birthday cards to honor his memory.[56]

Over the span of Henry's lifetime, he was especially loved by children. Over one hundred thirty years after his death, children are still learning his poems. "Paul Revere's Ride" and "The Village Blacksmith" have crept into our culture so much that people have made up their own words to these poems, often not realizing that Henry wrote the original words.

Children in the 1930s recited:

> Under the spreading chestnut tree
> The village smithy stands
> The muscles of his spindly arms
> Are strong as rubber bands.[57]

Children in the 1950s wrote in their autograph albums:

> Listen my children and you shall hear
> About the midnight ride of Sally dear
> First in a carriage, then on a wheel
> Now she rides in an automobile.[58]

And here is a song published in 1974:

> Under the spreading chestnut tree,
> When I held you on my knee,
> Oh, how happy we could be,
> Under the spreading chestnut tree.[59]

On February 25, 2007, the Henry Wadsworth Longfellow 200th Birthday Choral Concert took place at the First Parish Church of Portland, where

Henry used to pray as a child. Nearly twenty-four of his poems were sung by a chorus of eighty people, including different compositions of his poem "The Rainy Day" and selections from "The Song of Hiawatha," composed by Samuel Coleridge-Taylor.[60]

One month later, on March 25, 2007, another celebration was held at Sanders Theatre, in Cambridge, where Henry once spoke to schoolchildren while sharing the stage with the Children's Chair. Nine hundred people listened as the Boston Landmarks Orchestra played compositions of Henry's poems such as "Paul Revere's Ride," composed by Julian Wachner, with narration by the late senator Edward "Ted" Kennedy. Children from the Haggerty School Chorus sang Henry's poem "Snow-Flakes," composed by Lauren Bernofsky.[61]

Three months later, on July 15, 2007, another celebration to honor Henry's life was held on the lawn of the Longfellow House–Washington's Headquarters National Historic Site, where his children used to play. The Longfellow Chorus sang "The Village Blacksmith," composed by John Hatton, a friend of

Henry's. "From My Armchair" was sung by bass soloist John D. Adams.[62]

You can see more pictures of Henry and his family as well as drawings Henry made, a lock of hair from his wife Fanny, a lock of Henry's own hair, and the photograph of another letter from a child at the online Houghton Library exhibition curated by Christoph Irmscher titled *Public Poet, Private Man: Henry Wadsworth Longfellow at 200*, http://hcl.harvard.edu/libraries/houghton/exhibits/longfellow.

Perhaps Alfred W. Stockett from Mauch Chunk, Pennsylvania, now known as the town of Jim Thorpe, said it best on February 18, 1880, when he wrote *"I know that you are very busy, and receive a great many letters like mine, but as you are the childrens friend and poet, I hope you will not think it too much trouble to answer. . . ."*

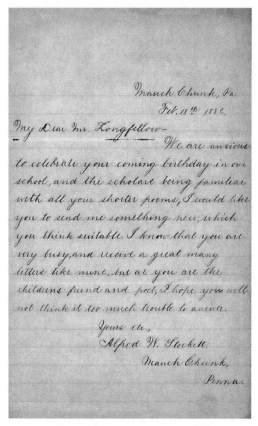

Figure 7.8. Photograph of Alfred W. Stockett's letter. [bMS Am 1340.7 Houghton Library, Harvard University.]

Figure 7.9. Henry Wadsworth Longfellow writing with a quill pen, circa 1862. Courtesy National Park Service, Longfellow House–Washington's Headquarters National Historic Site.

Acknowledgments

*M*y remarkable journey with Henry began in 1997 when I took a tour of the Longfellow National Historic Site, as it was called then, and was very moved to see the chair that the children of Cambridge gave to him in 1879. My discovery of the birthday letters at the Houghton Library allowed me to let the voices of children who loved him help me tell the story of his life. Without the assistance of the following people, I would not have been able to tell the story I set out to tell. I would like to thank Paul Blandford, former park guide, Longfellow House–Washington's Headquarters National Historic Site; Michele Clark, archivist at the Frederick Law

Olmstead National Historic Site, former archivist at the Longfellow House–Washington's Headquarters National Historic Site; Kelly Fellner, former supervisory park ranger at the Longfellow House–Washington's Headquarters National Historic Site; Janet Heywood, former director of Interpretive Programs, Mount Auburn Cemetery; the late Peggy Kaufman, former reference librarian at the Children's Literature Center, Library of Congress; Stephanie Philbrick, former research assistant, Maine Historical Society; Paula Rabkin, former research associate, Postal History, Headquarters, United States Postal Service; Kathleen Shea, former education coordinator, Maine Historical Society; Chris Smeriglio, former education assistant, Teach Maine Americorps, Maine Historical Society; Donald York, former archivist, Cambridge Public Library.

I would also like to thank Sean Casey, reference librarian, Rare Books and Manuscripts, Boston Public Library; Heather Cole, assistant curator of Modern Books and Manuscripts, Houghton Library, Harvard University; Kathleen P. Dunn, library assistant, Print

Department, Boston Public Library; Dani Fazio, images services coordinator, Maine Historical Society; Mary Catharine E. Johnsen, Special Collections and Design librarian, University Libraries, Carnegie Mellon University; Melanie Mahoney, reference librarian, Maine State Library; Kathy Peterson, archives assistant, George J. Mitchell Department of Special Collections and Archives, Bowdoin College Library; Jamie Kingman Rice, public services librarian, Maine Historical Society; Henry F. Scannell, curator, Microtext Department, Boston Public Library; James M. Shea, site manager and supervisory museum curator, Longfellow House–Washington's Headquarters National Historic Site; Liza Stearns, education specialist for the Frederick Law Olmstead National Historic Site, John F. Kennedy National Historic Site, and Longfellow House–Washington's Headquarters National Historic Site; Jane Winton, Print librarian, Boston Public Library.

I would especially like to thank Edward Copenhagen, Special Collections librarian, Monroe C. Gutman Library, Harvard Graduate School of

Education, Harvard University; Sarah Leroy, catalog librarian, University Library System, University of Pittsburgh; Alyssa K. Pacy, archivist, Cambridge Public Library Archives and Special Collections; Bridget McCormick, education coordinator, Maine Historical Society; Emilie Hardman, metadata and reference assistant, Houghton Library, Harvard University. I would like to thank the Hillman Library, University of Pittsburgh. I am also very grateful to the Carnegie Library of Pittsburgh and wish to thank Joanie Ejzak, librarian; Kathy Maron-Wood, senior librarian; Christi Miller, library assistant; Wes Roberts, senior librarian; and Denise Towarnicki, library assistant. I am particularly grateful for the efforts of Kathleen L. (Kit) Rawlins, assistant director, Cambridge Historical Commission, and Emily Walhout, reference assistant, Houghton Library, Harvard University. Above all, I want to deeply thank Anita Israel, archives specialist, Longfellow House–Washington's Headquarters National Historic Site.

Notes

Introduction: "Thank you so much for writing for children as well as grown folks, it makes us feel that we are not forgotten."

1. Publication of all letters from children to Henry Wadsworth Longfellow quoted in full or part, or photographed, is by permission of the Houghton Library, Harvard University. Shelf mark bMS Am1340.7, Henry Wadsworth Longfellow—Birthday Greetings.

2. *The Poetical Works of Longfellow*, with a new introduction by George Monteiro, based on the original Cambridge edition of 1893 prepared by Horace E. Scudder (Boston: Houghton Mifflin, 1975), pp. 14–15.

3. Information included by W. H. Bond, then curator of manuscripts at the Houghton Library, in the document *Letters to Henry Wadsworth Longfellow*, deposited in the Harvard College Library by the Trustees of the Longfellow House Trust, the Houghton Library, 1959. Purchased from the Trustees by Harvard in 1976.

4. Ibid.

5. Henry Wadsworth Longfellow—Birthday Greetings bMS Am 1340.7, Houghton Library, Harvard University, letter to Henry dated February 27, 1882, from Marshall, Missouri, and signed by Allen S. Newinay, Montague Condell, Henry Strother, Bell Chaffe, David Swisher, Leouna Cordello, and Lula Jester.

The walls of our schoolroom are decorated with lifesize portraits of you, Whittier, Bryant, Lowell and Holmes. Yours occupies the place of honor behind and over our teacher's desk and your kind eyes look down upon us all day, as we study.

6. Herbert S. Gorman, *A Victorian American: Henry Wadsworth Longfellow* (New York: George H. Doran, 1926), p. 351; Henry Wadsworth Longfellow, *The Children's Own Longfellow* (Boston: Houghton Mifflin, 1908), publishers' note.

7. Paula Rabkin, research associate, US Postal Service, telephone conversation with author, April 2000.

8. Anita Israel, archives specialist, Longfellow House–Washington's Headquarters National Historic Site, e-mail message to author, February 7, 2012.

9. George Lowell Austin, *Henry Wadsworth Longfellow—His Life, His Works, His Friendships* (Boston, 1883), pp. 374–76.

10. Annie Fields, *Authors and Friends* (Boston, 1897), p. 31.

11. Ibid., pp. 39–40.

12. Eleanor Hallowell Abbott, *Being Little in Cambridge When Everyone Else Was Big* (New York: D. Appleton-Century, 1936), p. 65.

13. Rhoda Cahn and William Cahn, *No Time for School, No Time for Work: The Story of Child Labor in America* (New York: Jullian Messner, 1972), p. 53.

14. Joel Spring, *The American School 1642–2000*, 5th ed. (New York: McGraw-Hill, 2001), pp. 220–24.

15. Ibid.

16. Report of Leroy F. Box, superintendent of education for the State of Alabama, *For the Scholastic Year ending 30th September, 1878, with Tabular Statistics of 1876–7. Containing also the Laws relating to the Public School System of the State, with an Appendix of Forms.* (Montgomery, Alabama, 1879), p. 22. Courtesy of Special Collections, Gutman Library, Harvard Graduate School of Education.

17. Spring, *American School 1642–2000*, p. 389.

18. Samuel Longfellow, ed., *Final Memorials of Henry Wadsworth Longfellow* (Boston, 1887), p. 295.

Chapter 1: "Tell me of something you did when you was a boy."

1. Joyce Butler, *Longfellow's Portland and Portland's Longfellow* (Portland: Maine Historical Society, 1987), p. 25.

2. Ibid., pp. 7, 22.

3. The census for Portland, Maine, for the year 1810 specifies that one "free white female 10 and under 16" and one "free white female 16 and under 26" lived in the Wadsworth-Longfellow House. Information provided by the Education Department, Maine Historical Society.

4. Lawrance Thompson, *Young Longfellow* (New York: Macmillan, 1938), p. 17.

5. Ibid.

6. Doris Ambler Porter, *A History of the Longfellow Garden* (Portland: Longfellow Garden Club, Maine Historical Society, 1983), p. 9; Annie Fields, *Authors and Friends* (Boston, 1897), p. 3.

7. Edward H. Elwell, "The Portland of Longfellow's Youth" in *Henry Wadsworth Longfellow Seventy-Fifth Birthday. Proceedings of the Maine Historical Society. February 27, 1882* (Portland, 1882), pp. 91–97; Newton Arvin, *Longfellow: His Life and Work* (Boston: Little, Brown, 1963), p. 5.

8. *The Poetical Works of Longfellow*, with a new introduction by George Monteiro, based on the Cambridge edition of 1893 prepared by Horace E. Scudder (Boston: Houghton Mifflin, 1975), pp. 193–95.

9. Butler, *Longfellow's Portland and Portland's Longfellow*, p. 22.

10. Thompson, *Young Longfellow*, pp. 15–16.

11. Butler, *Longfellow's Portland and Portland's Longfellow*, p. 25.

12. Samuel Longfellow, ed., *Life of Henry Wadsworth Longfellow: With Extracts from His Journals and Correspondence*, 3 vols. (Boston, 1891), 1:16.

13. Ibid., 1:16–17.

14. Quoted from certificate in bMS Am 1340 (166), Longfellow Materials on Childhood and Schooldays. Houghton Library, Harvard University.

15. Quoted from bMS Am 1340 (167), Longfellow—Copybook 1819. Houghton Library, Harvard University.

16. Thompson, *Young Longfellow*, p. 17.

17. Ibid., p. 14.

18. Ibid., pp. 19, 347.

19. Longfellow, *Life of Henry Wadsworth Longfellow*, 1:23.

20. Thompson, *Young Longfellow*, p. 30.

21. Ibid., p. 33.

22. Ibid., p. 34.

23. Ibid., p. 31.

24. Ibid., p. 39.

25. Ibid., pp. 41–45.

26. Ibid., p. 43.

27. Ibid., p. 58.

28. Ibid., p. 57.

29. Kathy Peterson, archives assistant, George J. Mitchell Department of Special Collections and Archives, Bowdoin College Library, e-mail message to author, January 10, 2012.

30. Thompson, *Young Longfellow*, p. 80.

31. Andrew Hilen, ed., *The Letters of Henry Wadsworth Longfellow*, 6 vols. (Cambridge, MA: Belknap Press of Harvard University, 1966), 1:150.

32. Thompson, *Young Longfellow*, p. 87.

Chapter 2: "I hope when I am a man I can write books."

1. Lawrance Thompson, *Young Longfellow* (New York: Macmillan, 1938), pp. 91–144, 377.

2. Ibid., p. 100.

3. Henry Wadsworth Longfellow, *Outre-Mer; A Pilgrimage beyond the Sea*, 2 vols. (New York, 1835), 1:61.

4. Ibid., 1:216–17.

5. Ibid., p. 217.

6. Newton Arvin, *Longfellow: His Life and Work* (Boston: Little, Brown, 1963), p. 24.

7. Longfellow, *Outre-Mer*, 2:164.

8. Ibid., 2:177–78.

9. Thomas Wentworth Higginson, *Old Cambridge* (New York: Macmillan, 1900), p. 118.

10. Thompson, *Young Longfellow*, pp. 193–94.

11. Ibid., p. 224.

12. *The Poetical Works of Longfellow*, with a new introduction by George Monteiro, based on the Cambridge edition of 1893 by Horace E. Scudder (Boston: Houghton Mifflin, 1975), p. 4.

13. Thompson, *Young Longfellow*, p. 234.

14. Ibid., pp. 234–37; Edward Wagenknecht, ed., *Mrs. Longfellow: Selected Letters and Journals of Fanny Appleton Longfellow* (New York: Longmans, Green, 1956), pp. 32–33.

15. Thompson, *Young Longfellow*, p. 240.

16. Ibid., p. 244.

17. Herbert G. Jones, *The Amazing Mr. Longfellow: Little Known Facts about a Well-Known Poet* (Portland, ME: Longfellow Press, 1957), p. 28.

18. Thomas Wentworth Higgenson, *Henry Wadsworth Longfellow* (Boston: Houghton Mifflin, 1902), pp. 118–19.

Chapter 3: "Tell me the names of your daughters and if they are all living."

1. Newton Arvin, *Longfellow: His Life and Work* (Boston: Little, Brown, 1963), p. 54.

2. Andrew Hilen, ed., *The Letters of Henry Wadsworth Longfellow*, 6 vols. (Cambridge, MA: Belknap Press of Harvard University Press, 1966), 2:487–88.

3. Ibid., p. 488.

4. Fanny Appleton Longfellow to Samuel Longfellow, February 13, 1845, in *Mrs. Longfellow: Selected Letters and Journals of Fanny Appleton Longfellow*, ed. Edward Wagenknecht (New York: Longmans, Green, 1956), p. 116; Fanny Appleton Longfellow to HWL, undated, in Wagenknecht, *Mrs. Longfellow*, pp. 116–17.

5. Henrietta Dana Skinner, *An Echo from Parnassus: Being Girlhood Memories of Longfellow and His Friends* (New York: J. H. Sears, 1928), pp. 21–22.

6. *The Poetical Works of Longfellow*, with a new introduction by George Monteiro, based on the Cambridge edition of 1893 prepared by Horace E. Scudder (Boston: Houghton Mifflin, 1975), p. 201.

7. Ernest Wadsworth Longfellow, *Random Memories* (Boston: Houghton Mifflin, 1922), p. 16. Ernest refers to the poem "Verses to a Child," but according to *The Poetical Works of Longfellow*, it is called "To a Child."

8. Edward Wagenknecht, *Henry Wadsworth Longfellow: Portrait of an American Humanist* (New York: Oxford University Press, 1966), p. 206.

9. Wagenknecht, *Mrs. Longfellow*, p. 147.

10. *Poetical Works of Longfellow*, p. 200.

11. Hilen, *Letters of Henry Wadsworth Longfellow*, 4:3.

12. Longfellow, *Random Memories*, p. 20.

13. Wagenknecht, *Henry Wadsworth Longfellow*, p. 148.

14. *Poetical Works of Longfellow*, p. 103.

15. Fanny Appleton Longfellow to Thomas G. Appleton, December 1849, in Wagenknecht, *Mrs. Longfellow*, p. 163.

16. Cambridge African American History Project, *The African American Experience in Cambridge, Teacher Resource Guide* (Cambridge, MA: privately printed, October 1994), unpaged. See timeline for 1855.

Chapter 4: "Which of your poems do you think is written the best?"

1. Samuel Longfellow, ed., *Life of Henry Wadsworth Longfellow: With Extracts from His Journals and Correspondence*, 3 vols. (Boston, 1891), 2:59.

2. *The Poetical Works of Longfellow*, with a new introduction by George Monteiro, based on the Cambridge edition of 1893 prepared by Horace E. Scudder (Boston: Houghton Mifflin, 1975), pp. 113–14.

3. Ernest Wadsworth Longfellow, *Random Memories* (Boston: Houghton Mifflin, 1922), pp. 13–14.

4. Andrew Hilen, ed., *The Letters of Henry Wadsworth Longfellow*, 6 vols. (Cambridge, MA: Belknap Press of Harvard University Press, 1972), 3:20.

5. Miss Alice Longfellow, "Longfellow with His Children," *Strand Magazine*, September 1897, p. 251.

6. Edward Wagenknecht, *Longfellow: A Full-Length Portrait* (New York: Longmans, Green, 1955), p. 116.

7. Anita Israel, archives specialist, Longfellow House–Washington's Headquarters National Historic Site, e-mail message to author, January 28, 2012. Henry's maroon smoking jacket is on site at Longfellow House–Washington's Headquarters National Historic Site.

8. Edward Waldo Emerson, *The Early Years of the Saturday Club* (Boston: Houghton Mifflin, 1918), p. 11.

9. Ibid., p. 12.

10. Longfellow, *Random Memories*, p. 36.

11. Longfellow, *Life of Henry Wadsworth Longfellow*, 3:357.

12. Fanny Appleton Longfellow to Mary Longfellow Greenleaf, August 1856, in *Mrs. Longfellow: Selected Letters and Journals of Fanny Appleton Longfellow*, ed. Edward Wagenknecht (New York: Longmans, Green, 1956), p. 166.

13. Anita Israel, archives specialist, Longfellow House–Washington's Headquarters National Historic Site, e-mail message to author, January 4, 2012. Both of Fanny's gowns described are on site at the Longfellow House–Washington's Headquarters National Historic Site.

14. Wagenknecht, *Mrs. Longfellow*, p. 205.

15. Ibid.

16. Courtesy National Park Service, Longfellow House–

Washington's Headquarters National Historic Site. According to the census reports, servants lived at 105 Brattle Street during the time that Henry lived there with his family.

17. Alice M. Longfellow, "A Sketch of Longfellow's Home Life," *Evangeline by Henry Wadsworth Longfellow with a Biographical Sketch, Introduction and Notes by H. E. Scudder,* Riverside Literature Series (Boston, 1896), p. xxxviii. Courtesy of Special Collections, Gutman Library, Harvard Graduate School of Education.

18. Longfellow, "Longfellow with His Children," p. 253.

19. Ibid.

20. HWL letter to Alice, July 26, 1860. Courtesy National Park Service, Longfellow House–Washington's Headquarters National Historic Site.

21. Longfellow, *Life of Henry Wadsworth Longfellow,* 2:417.

Chapter 5: "It was my cat's birthday yesterday."

1. Edward Wagenknecht, *Longfellow: A Full-Length Portrait* (New York: Longmans, Green, 1955), pp. 252–58.

2. Ibid., pp. 257–58.

3. Ibid., pp. 259–60.

4. Henrietta Dana Skinner, *An Echo from Parnassus: Being*

Girlhood Memories of Longfellow and His Friends (New York: J. H. Sears, 1928), pp. 92–101.

5. Information provided courtesy National Park Service, Longfellow House–Washington's Headquarters National Historic Site.

6. Skinner, *Echo from Parnassus*, p. 101.

7. Ibid., pp. 104–108.

8. Miss Alice Longfellow, "Longfellow with His Children," *Strand Magazine*, September 1897, p. 252.

9. Courtesy National Park Service, Longfellow House–Washington's Headquarters National Historic Site. June 1865, vol. 2 issue of *The Secret* featured a story about Trap, called "The Insult" written by Annie Allegra.

10. Newton Arvin, *Longfellow: His Life and Work* (Boston: Little, Brown, 1963), pp. 140–41.

11. Robert L. Gale, ed., *A Henry Wadsworth Longfellow Companion* (Westport, CT: Greenwood Press, 2003), p. 258.

12. *The Poetical Works of Longfellow*, with a new introduction by George Monteiro, based on the Cambridge edition of 1893 prepared by Horace E. Scudder (Boston: Houghton Mifflin, 1975), pp. 207–209.

13. Angela Sorby, *Schoolroom Poets: Childhood, Performance, and the Place of American Poetry, 1865–1917* (Durham: University of New Hampshire Press, 2005), pp. 15–16.

14. Henry Wadsworth Longfellow, *Paul Revere's Ride Together with Revere's Own Account* (Boston: Houghton Mifflin, 1907), pp. 49–76.

15. Ernest Wadsworth Longfellow, *Random Memories* (Boston: Houghton and Mifflin, 1922), pp. 69, 71.

16. HWL to Frances Farrar, December 28, 1863, in *The Letters of Henry Wadsworth Longfellow*, 6 vols., ed. Andrew Hilen (Cambridge, MA: Belknap Press of Harvard University Press, 1972), 4:376–77.

17. Longfellow, *Random Memories*, pp. 72–74.

18. Annie Fields, *Authors and Friends* (Boston, 1897), p. 18.

19. *Poetical Works of Longfellow*, p. 3.

20. Hilen, *Letters of Henry Wadsworth Longfellow*, 5:202. The governess Hannah Davie came along on the journey before visiting with her own family in England. Charley Longfellow came along and then went off on his own travels.

21. Ibid., 5:202–203.

22. Fields, *Authors and Friends*, pp. 35–36.

23. Ibid., p. 36.

Chapter 6: *"Our teacher read to us the poem about the blacksmith, and then told us about the children of Cambridge making you a present of a chair."*

1. Samuel Longfellow, ed., *Life of Henry Wadsworth Longfellow: With Extracts from His Journals and Correspondence*, 3 vols.

(Boston, 1891), 3:446–48; Edward A. Packard, "Dexter Pratt, 'The Village Smithy' of Longfellow's Poem" in *New England Essays: The Challenge of an Individualist* (Boston: Four Seas, 1929), pp. 71–74.

2. Longfellow, *Life of Henry Wadsworth Longfellow*, 3:447. Samuel mentions seven hundred names, but the author counted six hundred names in the book *The Children's Chair*.

3. Anita Israel, archives specialist, Longfellow House–Washington's Headquarters National Historic Site, e-mail message to author, February 7, 2012.

4. Catalog card 4469 pertaining to the Children's Chair given to Henry in 1879. Courtesy National Parks Service, Longfellow House–Washington's Headquarters National Historic Site.

5. Ibid.

6. Ibid.

7. Samuel Longfellow, ed., *Final Memorials of Henry Wadsworth Longfellow* (Boston: Ticknor, 1887), p. 284.

8. *The Poetical Works of Longfellow*, with a new introduction by George Monteiro, based on the Cambridge edition of 1893 prepared by Horace E. Scudder (Boston: Houghton Mifflin, 1975), p. 343.

9. Samuel Longfellow, "Longfellow and the Children" in *The Longfellow Remembrance Book: A Memorial for the Poet's Reader-Friends*, ed. Elbridge S. Brooks (Boston, 1888), p. 73.

10. Thomas Wentworth Higginson, *Old Cambridge* (New York: Macmillan, 1900), p. 142.

11. Thomas Wentworth Higginson, *Henry Wadsworth Longfellow* (Boston: Houghton Mifflin, 1902), p. 289–90.

12. *The Children's Chair* (book), catalog LONG 4473. Courtesy National Park Service, Longfellow House–Washington's Headquarters National Historic Site.

13. Phoebe Horsford to HWL, February 27, 1880, in Henry Wadsworth Longfellow Family Papers, LONG 27930. Courtesy National Park Service, Longfellow House–Washington's Headquarters National Historic Site.

14. City of Cambridge, *Report of the School Committee and the Report of the Superintendent of Schools for 1880* (Cambridge, 1881), pp. 26–27; "1630,–1880. Cambridge's Quarter Millenial. Great Success of the Celebration. The Children's Morning Exercises . . . ," *Cambridge Chronicle*, January 1, 1881, pp. 1–2. Courtesy of the Cambridge Public Library, Archives and Special Collections.

15. City Council, *Exercises in Celebrating the Two Hundred and Fiftieth Anniversary of the Settlement of Cambridge* (Cambridge, 1881), p. 16. Courtesy of the Cambridge Public Library, Archives and Special Collections.

16. Ibid., pp. 29–30.

17. Ibid.

18. George Lowell Austin, *Henry Wadsworth Longfellow—His Life, His Works, His Friendships* (Boston, 1883), p. 380.

Chapter 7: "We have a custom in our Public
                Schools of celebrating the birthdays
                of the great poets of the day."

1. Board of Education, *Part First: Fifty-First Annual Report for the School Year ending August 31, 1880 Board of Education, Cincinnati, Ohio, Report of Superintendent 1880–1881. Part Second: A Hand-Book for the School Year ending August 31, 1881* (Cincinnati, 1881), pp. 63–66. Courtesy of Special Collections, Gutman Library, Harvard University.

2. Andrew Hilen, ed., *The Letters of Henry Wadsworth Longfellow*, 6 vols. (Cambridge, MA: Belknap Press of Harvard University Press, 1982), 6:545.

3. Ibid. See HWL letter to John Peaslee, December 25, 1879.

4. Board of Education, *Part First* and *Part Second*, p. 64.

5. HWL to Carrie E. Middleton, January 29, 1880, in Hilen, *Letters of Henry Wadsworth Longfellow*, 6:559.

6. Alice M. Middleton's letter is in the collection of birthday greetings to Henry, bMS Am 1304.7, Houghton Library, Harvard University.

7. HWL to George Washington Greene, February 7, 1880, in Hilen, *Letters of Henry Wadsworth Longfellow*, 6:565–66.

8. Samuel Longfellow, ed., *Life of Henry Wadsworth Longfellow: With Extracts from His Journals and Correspondence*, 3 vols. (Boston, 1891), 3:448.

9. Ibid., 3:321. See HWL to William Senter, Cambridge, January 12, 1882.

10. Ibid., 3:312.

11. Ibid.

12. Ibid.

13. bMS Am 1340.7 Houghton Library, Harvard University.

14. Ibid.

15. "Old Cambridge," *Cambridge Chronicle,* March 5, 1881, p. 1.

16. HWL to George Washington Greene, November 28, 1881, in *Final Memorials of Henry Wadsworth Longfellow,* ed. Samuel Longfellow (Boston, 1897), p. 305.

17. Hilen, *Letters of Henry Wadsworth Longfellow,* 6:768–81.

18. Ibid., 6:676. See HWL to George Washington Greene, Cambridge, March 14, 1882.

19. "Old Cambridge," *Cambridge Chronicle,* March 4, 1882, p. 2.

20. Ibid.

21. This is the first verse and the last two verses of Bessie Mifflin's poem. The poem is in the HWL birthday greetings collection bMS Am 1340.7 Houghton Library, Harvard University.

22. HWL to Bessie Mifflin, March 16, 1882, in Longfellow, *Life of Henry Wadsworth Longfellow,* 3:322.

23. Ibid., 3:324–25.

24. Ibid., 3:325.

25. Ibid.

26. Ibid.

27. "Longfellow, Dead," *Cambridge Chronicle*, March 25, 1882, p. 4.

28. George Lowell Austin, *Henry Wadsworth Longfellow—His Life, His Works, His Friendships* (Boston, 1883), p. 389.

29. "Longfellow, Dead," p. 4.

30. Austin, *Henry Wadsworth Longfellow*, p. 392.

31. Common Schools of Cincinnati, *Part First Fifty-Third Annual Report for the School Year ending August 31, 1882* (Cincinnati, 1883), p. 89. Courtesy of Special Collections, Gutman Library, Harvard Graduate School of Education.

32. Alfred S. Roe, *American Authors and Their Birthdays*, Riverside Series (Boston, 1887), first p. of preface.

33. Josephine E. Hodgdon, comp., *Leaflets from Standard Authors—Longfellow: Poems and Prose Passages from the Works of Henry Wadsworth Longfellow for Reading and Recitation* (Boston, 1891), p. 7. Courtesy of Special Collections, Gutman Library, Harvard Graduate School of Education.

34. Anita Israel, archives specialist, Longfellow House–Washington's Headquarters National Historic Site, telephone conversation with author, February 8, 2012.

35. Samuel Longfellow, ed., *Life of Henry Wadsworth Longfellow: With Extracts from His Journals and Correspondence*, 3 vols. (Boston, 1891), 3:346–51.

36. Longfellow Statue Coll. vol. 2. Coll. 1547 Coll. of Maine Historical Society; *Exercises at the Unveiling of the Statue of*

Henry Wadsworth Longfellow: Portland, Maine, September 29, 1888 (Portland, 1888).

37. Writers' Program of the Work Progress Administration in the State of Maine, *Portland City Guide* (Portland, ME: Forest City Printing, 1940), p. 273; *Exercises at the Unveiling of the Statue of Henry Wadsworth Longfellow: Portland, Maine, September 29, 1888* (Portland, 1888), inside front cover, pp. 7–8.

38. Coll. S-6517, Misc. box 203/11; Coll. S-7160, Misc. box 244/17, Coll. of Maine Historical Society.

39. "Ladies' Committee. Report of an Organization That Worked Successfully for the Longfellow Centenary," *Cambridge Tribune*, April 6, 1907, p. 8. Longfellow Scrapbook, courtesy of the Cambridge Public Library, Archives and Special Collections.

40. "Honoring Memory of Poet of Craigie House: Lovers of Longfellow Show Their Esteem on Anniversary of His Birth, Children Cry Because They Are Unable to Attend Exercises in Theater," *Boston Journal*, February 28, 1907. Courtesy Microtext Department, Boston Public Library.

41. Ibid.

42. *The Henry Wadsworth Longfellow Memorial Statue. Exercises at the Unveiling, May 7, 1909, in Washington, DC* (Boston: Southgate Press, copyright 1909 by the Longfellow National Memorial Association), p. 7.

43. Winthrop S. Scudder, *The Longfellow Memorial Association 1882–1922, An Historical Sketch* (Cambridge, MA: Cosmos Press, 1922).

44. Ibid.

45. "New Stamp Honoring Poet Ready for Public Feb 16," *Portland Sunday Telegram*, February 4, 1940; "Longfellow Stamps Sold Here Today by the Thousands," *Portland Evening Express*, February 16, 1940. Collections of the Maine Historical Society, Longfellow Scrapbook Coll. 1951, vol. 2.

46. Anita Israel, archives specialist, Longfellow House–Washington's Headquarters National Historic Site, e-mail message to author February 6, 2012.

47. James A. Shea, site manager and supervisory museum curator, Longfellow House–Washington's National Historic Site, telephone conversation and e-mail message to author, December 5, 2011.

48. Ibid.

49. Catalog card 4469 pertaining to the Children's Chair given to Henry in 1879. Courtesy of the National Park Service, Longfellow House–Washington's Headquarters National Historic Site.

50. Members of the Hannah Winthrop Chapter, Daughters of the American Revolution, comps., *An Historic Guide to Cambridge* (Cambridge, MA, 1907), p. 89; Robert Bell Rettig, *Guide to Cambridge Architecture: Ten Walking Tours* (Cambridge, MA, 1969), unpaged, tour C, site no. 3; Sarah Zimmerman, *Landmark Designation Study Report for 54 Brattle Street, Dexter Pratt House* (Cambridge Historical Commission, October 21, 1988).

51. Janet Heywood, former director of Interpretive Programs, Mount Auburn Cemetery, Cambridge, MA, conversation

with author, May 2000; Anita Israel, archives specialist, Longfellow House–Washington's Headquarters National Historic Site, telephone conversation with author, November 22, 2011.

52. Kathleen Shea, former education coordinator, Maine Historical Society, conversation with author, June 2000; Bridget McCormick, education coordinator, Maine Historical Society, e-mail message to author November 29, 2011.

53. Laura Fecych Sprague, "Rethinking Restoration at the Wadsworth-Longfellow House," *Early American Life,* February 2004, pp. 46–53; Ray Routhier, "This Old House," *Portland Press Herald,* September 18, 2000, pp. 1C, 3C; *The Wadsworth-Longfellow House: Restoring "The Old Original,"* fact sheet pertaining to the Wadsworth-Longfellow House Centennial Restoration, Maine Historical Society, 2001, Courtesy of the Maine Historical Society; Bridget McCormick, education coordinator, Maine Historical Society, e-mail message to author, December 21, 2011.

54. Routhier, "This Old House," p. 3C.

55. Bridget McCormick, education coordinator, Maine Historical Society, e-mail message to author, December 21, 2011.

56. Shea, conversation with author, June 2000; McCormick, e-mail message to author, November 29, 2011.

57. Peggy Kaufman, former reference librarian, Children's Literature Center, Library of Congress, conversation with author, May 2000.

58. Lillian Morrison, *Yours Till Niagara Falls, A Collection of Autograph Verses* (New York: Thomas Y. Crowell, 1950), p. 142.

59. Virginia Tashjian, *With a Deep Sea Smile: Story Hour Stretches for Large or Small Groups* (Boston: Little, Brown, 1974), p. 122.

60. "Celebrating Henry Wadsworth Longfellow's Bicentennial," *Longfellow House Bulletin: A Newsletter of the Friends of the Longfellow House and the National Park Service* 2, no.1 (2007): 7.

61. Ibid., p. 1.

62. Ibid., p. 7.

Index

References to illustrations and photographs are in **bold**. Where appropriate, some subentries are listed chronologically rather than alphabetically.